Penguins of the Falkland Islands and South America

by
Dr. Mike Bingham

First published in 2001 by Environmental Research Unit
Publications, Stanley, Falkland Islands

ISBN: 0-75963-335-5

This book is printed on acid free paper.

1stBooks – rev. 05/07/01

LIST OF CONTENTS

Preface v

PART 1: An Introduction to Penguins 1

PART 2: Diversity of the Species 21

    King Penguin *(Aptenodytes patagonicus)* 23

    Gentoo Penguin (*Pygoscelis papua*) 29

    Southern Rockhopper (*Eudyptes c. chrysocome*) 38

    Macaroni Penguin *(Eudyptes chrysolophus)* 48

    Magellanic Penguin *(Spheniscus magellanicus)* 52

    Humboldt Penguin *(Spheniscus humboldti)* 62

    Galapagos Penguin *(Spheniscus mendiculus)* 67

PART 3: Penguins and the Environment 73

PART 4: Bibliography 91

Glossary 129

Index 131

PREFACE

My interest in penguins was sparked off when I was about seven years old, and I saw my first live penguin at Dudley Zoo. I was immediately fascinated by these comical birds, that looked so out of place in the real world, and seemed more akin to cartoon characters. Even as I grew older, it seemed hard to accept penguins as real wild animals: creatures that were able to hold their own in a harsh and dangerous environment. The more I learned about them, the more fascinated I became.

This childhood fascination with penguins fuelled my fight to save them, when in 1993 I was appointed Conservation Officer for the Falkland Islands, a position which brought me into conflict with the Falkland Islands Government and local business interests. In 1995 I led an island-wide penguin census which revealed huge population declines. Between 1984 and 1995 penguin populations in the Falklands had crashed to less than 20% of their former size, and the evidence pointed towards commercial fishing as the culprit.

The Falkland Islands Government insisted that the declines were part of a global trend, so in 1996 I led a penguin census in nearby Chile and Argentina, where the two species in greatest decline held the remainder of their world population. This census showed that these species had not declined in South America, and that the crash in penguin numbers was a problem restricted to the Falklands.

I was asked to cover up my findings, and when I refused to do so I was replaced as Conservation Officer. I set up the Environmental Research Unit, and continued my penguin research using independent funding. In 1998 oil exploration began in the Falklands, and poor environmental protection led to three separate oil spills, killing hundreds of penguins and other seabirds. I protested about the lack of environmental safeguards, and the unnecessary damage being done to Falklands wildlife by the Falkland Islands Government. The Falkland Islands

Government decided that my research posed a threat to future wealth from fishing and oil development, and began a campaign to remove me.

Firstly I discovered firearms hidden under my bed, but I was able to dispose of them prior to the Customs raid which followed. Then I was arrested on charges of deception, but released when the Police were forced to admit they had fabricated the evidence. The official explanation for fabricating evidence was "administrative error". Then the Falkland Islands Government tried to deport me, claiming that I had criminal convictions for burglary, which I didn't. The government were eventually forced to admit that they had used convictions belonging to a totally different person, and that another "administrative error" had occurred.

When I was arrested yet again, I turned to Amnesty International, who put me in touch with Index on Censorship. They exposed the corruption within the Falkland Islands Government, and the story hit the British newspapers in October 1999.

The Sunday Times, The Guardian, The Observer, The Daily Post and Birdwatch magazine all published the story, with titles such as "Arrested, framed, threatened - Researcher fights a one-man war in the Falklands". The British Government sent a Police & Criminal Justice Advisor to conduct an investigation, and within 24 hours of his arrival I received an apology from the Chief of Police, and assurances that such things would never happen again.

Unfortunately this has only meant a change in tactics. After harassing my wife and 10 year old child to the point where they were forced to flee to Chile, the Falklands government have begun attempts to revoke my residency status on the grounds that I have no knowledge or skills of use to the islands. With a PhD in Environmental Surveying, Monitoring and Conservation, I apparently have no place monitoring the health of the world's most important penguin breeding site.

Despite their 4 year campaign of harassment, the Falkland Islands Government have been forced to accept the reality of the penguin decline, and since my penguin census was conducted in 1995, annual fishing effort has been reduced. Since then Gentoo and Rockhopper penguin populations have stopped declining, and now seem to have reached an equilibrium, albeit at a much lower level than before fishing began. Unfortunately Magellanic Penguins are still declining in the Falklands, and my research is now concentrating on identifying the cause, with support from the Chilean government.

I would like to offer special thanks to: Environmental Research Unit Ltd., Charles Darwin Research Station, Wellcome Foundation, Royal Air Force, British Forces Falkland Islands, Aerovias DAP, Tercera Zona Naval, Universidad de Magallanes, Instituto de la Patagonia, CONAF, Parque Nacional Galápagos, Hernan Vargas, Claudio Venegas, Nicolás Soto, Elena Mejias, Dee Boersma, Ricardo Fuentes, and all the landowners whose property I have visited during my research.

PART 1: An Introduction to Penguins

Dr. Mike Bingham

The first bird to be named a penguin was not in fact a penguin at all, but a Great Auk. The word came from the Welsh "pen gwyn", which means white head. Although the Great Auk belonged to the auk family, it was flightless and similar in appearance to true penguins. Being flightless, and therefore easy to catch for food, the Great Auk was hunted to extinction by sailors in the 19th Century. When sailors later encountered similar flightless birds in the southern hemisphere they also called them penguins, since when the name has been used to describe flightless birds belonging to the family *Spheniscidae.*

World-wide there are 17 species of penguin, all of which breed in the Southern hemisphere. Three of the five species which breed in the Falkland Islands, also breed in South America, but the Pacific waters of South America also hold two further species which are found nowhere else in the world.

Penguins differ from birds which are able to fly, by having a much heavier and more robust skeleton. Birds that fly must have a skeleton which is as light as possible, in order to make flight possible. This is achieved through bones that are paper-thin or hollow, often with internal honeycombing that combines adequate strength with low weight. For flying birds that also dive, such as Auks, this low density skeleton means that birds must work hard to overcome considerable natural buoyancy when diving below the water surface. For penguins that do not have the power of flight, such light weight skeletons hold no advantage, and they therefore have bones which are considerably denser, giving greater strength and reduced buoyancy.

The penguin skeleton is also markedly different from other birds around the furcula and breast bone, due to the differing movement and muscular requirements of penguin flippers compared to bird wings. Such differences in bone structure provide vital clues to the ancestry of penguins, since bones are often the only parts that remain as fossils.

In 1861, the fossilised skeleton of a bird-like creature was found in a limestone quarry near Solnhofen, southern Germany. Given the name *Archaeopteryx lithographica,* it was considered to be the missing link between birds and their reptilian ancestors, dating back 150 million years. Archaeopteryx had both wings and feathers, but was still reptilian in many other ways, and was too heavy to fly. It probably lived in woodlands and used its wings to aid short glides from tree to tree, gaining height once more by climbing up through the branches with the help of the claws on its wings.

Throughout the Cretaceous Period, evolution reduced the skeletal weight, and modified the bones and muscles of the wings, furcula and breast bone, until true birds with the power of flight took to the skies to seek an abundance of insect prey. It is generally believed that this radiation of birds took place about 65 million years ago following the demise of the dinosaurs.

It is also believed that penguins evolved sometime after this radiation, from birds that had the power of flight, although this is by no means certain. The first penguin fossil to be discovered was that of *Palaeeudyptes antarcticus,* found in rocks that were around 25 million years old, in New Zealand during the 19th century. Since then penguin fossils have been found that date back around 50 million years, which show many of the typical features associated with modern penguins. No penguin fossils have ever been found in the northern hemisphere. The largest penguin ever to have been discovered was similar in size to a man.

Despite a long evolutionary history, today's species have much in common. They mostly have blackish upperparts and whitish underparts on both the abdomen and flippers. This helps to camouflage the penguin against the lighter sky when viewed from below, and the darker waters when viewed from above, making them harder to spot by both predators and prey. The feathers are waterproof and interlocking, providing an effective barrier to water. Each feather has small muscles which allow them to be held tightly down against the body whilst swimming, to form a thin water proof layer. Little air is therefore trapped in the plumage when swimming, preventing excessive buoyancy which would hinder diving. When on land, these muscles hold the feathers erect, thereby trapping a thick layer of warm air to provide the best insulation against cold wind.

The insulation provided by the plumage is further aided by thick fat deposits beneath the skin, and a counter-current blood supply to the exposed legs and feet. The blood vessels supplying warm blood to the legs and feet are surrounded by the vessels returning cooler blood back to the body, enabling much of the heat lost from the warm blood to be recovered. This vascular system is also able to severely restrict the amount of blood flowing to the flippers and feet, which may be kept as cool as 6 degrees celsius despite a body core temperature of 39 degrees celsius. This considerably reduces the amount of heat lost during cold weather, but the process can also be reversed so as to aid heat loss during hot weather.

Penguins also have a counter-current heat exchange system in the nasal passages, whereby air from inhalation and expiration are mixed in a common chamber. This allows recovery of much of the heat lost from the blood capillaries during respiration. This process can however be reversed to aid heat loss during periods of hot weather.

Air is a poor conductor of heat, and all adult penguins in the Falkland Islands and South America, are able to maintain their body temperatures on land without the need to increase metabolic activity. By contrast, water is a very effective conductor of heat, and despite their adaptations most penguins do rely on increased metabolic activity to maintain their body temperature at sea. In the comparatively warmer waters around the Falkland Islands and South America however, the increased metabolic activity resulting from swimming and foraging is sufficient to meet these needs.

By comparison to adults, chicks have very different types of plumage, which serve completely different purposes. Newly hatched chicks have a protoptile plumage, which is very sparse, and provides inadequate insulation from the cold. However, at this period of development chicks do not require insulation, because they are brooded by the adult, and the sparse plumage enables rapid transfer of heat from the adult brood patch to the chick. Only when chicks near the end of the brood period, do they need a plumage with greater insulative properties.

As chicks grow larger, and demand more food, it is necessary for both adults to go to sea to forage. Prior to being left by both adults, chicks grow a thick, fluffy plumage called the mesoptile plumage, which traps a thick layer of air and provides excellent insulation. This plumage provides better insulation against cold wind than the adult plumage, however it is not waterproof and is only effective when dry. Normally this is not a problem, since chicks do not enter the water at this stage. The insulation properties of the mesoptile plumage can be seen in breeding colonies during periods of hot weather when chicks often suffer from heat stress. By contrast, the breakdown of this insulation when wet is evident during periods of heavy rain, when some chicks can become saturated, and die from hypothermia.

Despite these drawbacks, the mesoptile plumage provides the best possible compromise under a wide range of climatic conditions. Its development coincides with other physiological changes, which enable the chick to regulate its own body temperature without the need for being brooded. When the chick becomes fully developed, further physiological changes occur, and the mesoptile plumage is shed and replaced by a waterproof plumage similar to that of the adults. This plumage needs to be kept waterproof in order to maintain an adequate level of insulation at sea, and in order to retain these properties, the plumage must be renewed regularly throughout adult life. This is usually performed during an annual moult, when birds come ashore for a period of 2 - 4 weeks, while the old feathers are pushed out by the new ones growing from underneath.

Adults suffer from greater levels of heat loss during their annual moult, as a result of the breakdown of the plumage. They are able to partially compensate for this by increasing their subcuticular fat deposits prior to moulting, which occurs during a period of intensive feeding at sea. Nevertheless adults must then come ashore to undertake the moult, since the plumage loses its waterproofing qualities during the moult, and would become waterlogged. The birds are unable to re-enter the water again until all the new feathers have grown in, and their plumage is entirely waterproof once again. Since their food is caught entirely at sea, it means that a period of fasting is required during the moult period.

During normal fasting, such as during periods of incubation or brooding, penguins are able to reduce their metabolic activity in order to reduce the rate at which body fat reserves are used. However, during the moulting period they are unable to do this, since the reduced insulation resulting from losing feathers, creates a need for additional metabolic activity to maintain body temperature. Some additional energy is also required for the growth of new feathers, and proteins must be broken down to provide essential amino acids for the synthesis of the new feathers.

The waterproofing qualities of the adult plumage is maintained by constant preening. A waxy substance is produced from the uropygial gland at the base of the tail, and this is spread onto the feathers during preening to maintain their waterproofing qualities. Preening also realigns the feathers, which interlock through microscopic hooks. Plumage around the eyes and head can only be preened by the feet, so penguins may often be seen preening each other around these areas. This is called allopreening, and it not only allows the preening of inaccessible areas, but also forms part of the pair bonding behaviour. Not all penguin species allopreen however.

All penguins look rather ungainly on land, but in the water they are truly graceful. Evolution has made their wings small and sturdy in order to "fly" in the dense medium of water, but these adaptations have meant the loss of flight in air. In water, penguins use their flippers with much the same action as other birds do in air, using their tails and webbed feet for steering and braking. Penguins can reach speeds of up to 14km. per hour in short bursts, although half this is a more normal cruising speed.

The need to breathe while swimming means that penguins often swim using a porpoising action; travelling just below the surface and periodically leaping above the surface to take short breaths without slowing. This is the quickest mode of travel, and the preferred technique of Rockhoppers and Macaronis, which can average 10km per hour for prolonged periods.

An alternative technique is to travel below the surface for periods of up to 2 minutes, followed by a short surface rest of up to 30 seconds. Average speeds of up to 6km per hour can be attained using this technique, and it is the preferred mode of travel for Gentoos and Magellanics, unless pursued by predators. It has often been claimed that penguins porpoise when pursued by predators, because leaping from the water confuses predators. This may be true, but it is equally feasible that penguins porpoise simply because it is the fastest means of escape.

The penguin body is the perfect shape for reducing drag under water and is unmatched by any man-made design. The drag co-efficient of the penguin body is so low, that despite its very much greater size, a penguin the size of a Gentoo creates less drag through the water than a £1 coin. This is of great significance for research scientists wishing to attach devices to penguins in order to study penguin behaviour. Even very small devices may greatly increase the drag co-efficient of the penguin, requiring it to exert much more energy during swimming, and therefore affecting both behaviour and results.

Penguins dive in search of prey, and then having located it they chase it, and swallow it whole under water. To locate and capture prey therefore requires good underwater vision, but the differing refractive indexes of water and air require different shaped lenses. Penguins therefore are able to alter the shape of the lens considerably, enabling them to compensate for the differences in refractive index, and allowing good vision in air and water.

Penguins generally feed during daylight hours. Even at depth, sufficient light still penetrates to allow them to locate their prey, especially when searching from below where prey are silhouetted against the light from above. Even so, light at the blue-green end of the spectrum penetrates to much greater depths than reds and yellows, it is therefore unsurprising that penguin eyes are more sensitive to blue-green wavelengths.

King Penguins are known to forage at night-time, although such foraging dives tend to be very shallow. The main prey of King Penguins are bioluminous Lantern Fish, and the bioluminescence of these fish may allow the penguins to locate them in the absence of daylight.

The diet of most penguins consists of varying proportions of fish, cephalopods and crustaceans, determined by variations in local abundance and by the size of prey each penguin species can swallow. Penguins also swallow small stones, and it is likely that these help in mechanically breaking up the food in the stomach.

It is often supposed that prey, such as fish and squid, are more or less evenly distributed throughout the water, but that is not generally the case. Rather like herds of wildebeest or antelope on an Africa plain, fish and squid group together in high concentrations, with only low concentrations being found in the surrounding ocean. Penguins are therefore not so much seeking individual prey when they begin to forage, but rather searching for patches with a high concentration of prey where they will remain to feed. These patches tend to move around, but are generally found within a particular area at certain times of year.

During chick-rearing, few species forage more than 40km from their nest-site in search of food. Breeding sites are therefore situated near to areas of high prey concentration. The result of this is that very large colonies, for example Rockhopper colonies, have so many penguins feeding in these few areas, that competition is high. Breeding success, and in turn the population size of colonies, is often very dependent upon the amount of food available within these critical areas. Clearly any long-term reduction in prey abundance within these areas is likely to result in population decline.

Different species of penguin favour different prey, and the depths to which they dive is related to the location of such prey. All penguins are capable of diving to depths of 100m, but the larger penguins, such as King Penguins, can dive to depths of over 300m. The pressure exerted on the penguin's body increases by one atmosphere for every 10m depth, penguins therefore need a number of physiological adaptations to enable them to dive to such great depths.

The main problem penguins face is being unable to breathe underwater. Having a relatively small body size compared to seals and cetaceans, penguins are more restricted in the amount of oxygen that they can store to sustain them during underwater dives. The underwater pressure compresses the air held in the lungs and air-sacs, and consequently these airways only provide about a third of the oxygen requirements needed for each dive.

The haemoglobin in red blood cells holds a certain amount of oxygen in all animals, in order to circulate oxygen from the lungs to all parts of the body. In penguins, the blood has a much higher concentration of haemoglobin than is necessary solely for circulatory needs, and this is used as an oxygen store during underwater dives. In addition the muscle tissues have high concentrations of myoglobin, which also stores oxygen in the very place that it is most needed for underwater swimming.

Water becomes colder with increasing depth, and during foraging dives the core body temperature of penguins can decrease substantially as a result of heat loss, and the ingestion of cold food and water. This cooling of the body core also helps to reduce the oxygen requirement during dives, by suppressing the metabolic activity of organs that are not required for foraging.

As oxygen is used up during respiration, carbohydrates and fats are burned off to provide energy, and the by-product of this process is carbon dioxide. During underwater dives this carbon dioxide builds up in the blood stream due to the lack of fresh air entering the lungs and air-sacs. Under normal circumstances this excess carbon dioxide would combine with the blood to become carbonic acid, raising the acidity of the blood. It is actually the build up of carbon dioxide which causes the sensation of suffocation, rather than the lack of oxygen. Even small increases in the acidity of the blood can be metabolically damaging, and penguins therefore have an ability to buffer the blood, preventing the blood from becoming too acidic in the presence of increased levels of carbon dioxide.

Even despite these adaptations, penguins are often unable to hold sufficient oxygen to sustain the deepest dives, and they have therefore evolved physiological adaptations that enable them to use anaerobic respiration (the production of energy in the absence of oxygen). In humans, when muscles become overworked and lack sufficient oxygen to sustain their energy requirements, the build up of lactic acid resulting from anaerobic respiration quickly causes pain and muscle fatigue. In penguins however, the muscle tissues contain high levels of an enzyme called lactate dehydrogenase which allows muscles to continue working anaerobically, by neutralising the build up of lactic acid. This lactic acid is later expelled from the body when normal breathing is resumed, during periods of surface rest or shallow diving.

Penguins must all come ashore in order to breed, and the sites they choose for this vary considerably between species. Some species remain around the breeding colonies throughout the year, whilst others desert the colonies completely during the non-breeding season. The latter species generally remain at sea throughout the non-breeding season, and their foraging ranges are often difficult to determine during this period. Pre-breeding birds of most species also tend to remain at sea, except during their annual moult.

Some penguin species may commence breeding when just 2 years old, while other species do not breed until 6 or more years of age In most species the males arrive at the breeding site a few days before the females, and this is due to the fact that there are more males than females. Despite popular belief, most penguins are not faithful for life, and the rules of partnership are complex.

Both partners generally return to the same breeding site each year, and many species use the same actual nest, which they refurbish each season. The male usually seeks out his previous partner in order to breed with her once more, but if the female arrives at the nest site first, and cannot find her previous mate, she will quickly pair with any unattached male nearby.

This makes sense, since if she delays breeding too long for a mate that may never arrive, she is likely to loose her opportunity to breed that season. It is therefore essential that the male arrives at the nest site before the female, since it is much harder for an unpaired male to find a replacement female, and he cannot run the risk of losing his previous partner.

On occasions a female may arrive at the nest site first, and not finding her previous mate will proceed to copulate with another male, only to reform her partnership with the previous years partner when he finally appears. This leaves her unsuspecting partner to incubate and rear the offspring of another male. This is an added incentive for the male to arrive first, in order to ensure that his partner does not attempt to copulate with any other males.

Pair bonding is reinforced, and new partnerships formed, by ritualised displays and nest building. Penguins display a number of behavioural rituals to display territorial defence, aggression, submission, and to enhance the pair bonding. Such rituals include head and flipper waving, bowing, presenting gifts, allopreening, and vocal calls. Aggressive postures are designed to avoid the need for physical contact, but fights do still break out within the colony during the establishment of mates and territories. Such fights can be aggressive, with birds using bills and flippers against their rival. Birds generally defend a territory within pecking distance of their nest.

Mating takes place within a few days, and most species lay two eggs at an interval of around 4 days. Breeding in colonies allows synchrony of egg laying, which in turn reduces the sustainability of eggs and young for dependent predators which are also trying to raise young. More evenly aged colonies are also easier to defend, since they offer less opportunity for predators to prey on younger chicks. Penguin colonies are sometimes incorrectly called "rookeries", a term which actually refers only to breeding colonies of rooks, a member of the crow family.

Both parents take turns to incubate the eggs and care for the chicks once they have hatched. An area of skin on the lower abdomen lacks feathers, and is called the brood patch. This allows sufficient transfer of heat to eggs and small chicks as the bird lies over them in the nest. During incubation, the brood pouch becomes swollen and diffused with blood to aid heat transfer. When the birds are not incubating, the patch can be closed, so that the feathers around it join and exclude water during feeding periods at sea.

Prior to hatching, the chicks call to their parents from inside the egg. The chicks use a small point on the tip of the bill, called the egg tooth, to break through the egg shell. Hatching can often be a prolonged process, lasting a couple of days.

When the chicks reach about two weeks of age, the original protoptile plumage, which is thin and readily transmits warmth from the parent bird, is replaced by a thicker mesoptile plumage. This provides good insulation, and in association with metabolic changes, it allows the chick to maintain its own body temperature. This allows both parents to go to sea in search of food, in order to meet the growing demand for food from the larger chicks. In most surface-nesting species, chicks whose parents are at sea form into creches, and this provides them with a certain degree of protection from cold weather and predators.

Returning adults identify their chicks by recognition of their distinctive calls. Chicks must beg for food in order to initiate a feeding response from the parent, and this is usually done by constant pecking around the parents bill. Penguins, unlike most other birds, do not have crops and regurgitate partially digested food directly from the stomach. Generally it is the adults who must be convinced that they are receiving feeding demands from their own chick, since hungry chicks will happily beg from any passing adult, or even other chicks.

Mortality amongst chicks is generally quite high, and varies from species to species according to different breeding strategies. Some species lay only one egg, or lay two eggs of different size, concentrating all their efforts into raising just one healthy chick. Such species are generally longer-lived, do not begin breeding until several years of age, and use a strategy of slow reproduction but lower adult mortality. Species adopting such a strategy often show lower annual fluctuations in breeding success and population size. Nevertheless, lower reproductive rates mean that they are slower to recover from population crashes or human exploitation.

Other species lay two equally sized eggs, and put equal effort into rearing both. This allows them to achieve very high reproductive rates during seasons of high food abundance, but they may also suffer from low reproductive rates when food is scarce. These species tend to be shorter lived, begin breeding at an early age, and use a strategy of rapid reproduction but variable adult mortality. Such species tend to show high annual fluctuations in both breeding success and population size. Because they can achieve high reproductive rates, they are perhaps more able to recover from natural disasters and direct exploitation, but would still be vulnerable to a long-term reduction in food abundance.

When chicks are ready to leave the nest site and take to the sea, they shed their mesoptile plumage and develop their adult waterproof plumage, allowing them to enter the water for the first time. The term "fledging" normally applies to the stage when young birds take their first flight from the nest, but in penguins the term refers to chicks changing into adult plumage. Some parental responsibility may still remain after fledging, but before long most adult penguins return to the sea in order to build up their body fat reserves in preparation for their annual moult.

These foraging trips usually last up to about four weeks, and allow the build up of thicker layers of sub-cuticular fat, which will provide better heat insulation during the forthcoming moult. This is particularly important, since adults are unable to feed during their 2 - 4 week moult period, and must sustain heat loss by burning up body fat. If insufficient body fat exists, adults may starve to death prior to completion of their moult. In practice this very rarely happens, but it has been observed following seasons of extreme food shortage, such as following the effects of El Niño Southern Oscillations (ENSO).

Healthy adult penguins have few natural predators on land, although on occasions Sea Lions have been known to come ashore to take adult penguins. At sea however, penguins are often killed by Leopard Seals, Sea Lions and Killer Whales. Skuas and gulls are regular predators of eggs and small chicks during the breeding season, but are unable to over-power healthy adults.

Penguins are the major avian top-predators in the southern oceans. The entire world population of all penguins consume around 20 - 25 million tons of fish, squid and crustaceans every year. By way of comparison, the world's commercial fisheries remove around 70 million tons per year. However, because penguins breed in very large numbers at particular sites, and generally forage within a range of 40km, there is considerable local competition for food. Breeding colonies therefore rely on highly productive feeding areas within their daily foraging range, in order to sustain chick production. Any significant reduction in food abundance within this foraging zone is likely to have adverse affects on chick-rearing ability.

This makes such areas particularly susceptible to commercial fishing operations, which are also trying to target the same highly productive feeding areas. This situation is exacerbated when commercial fishing takes place just prior to or during the breeding season, as is currently the case in the Falkland Islands. Even if fishing is managed in a sustainable manner, the results of such timing can be very detrimental. A reduction of prey in these all important foraging areas, at a time when penguins are unable to forage further afield, and when extra food is required for chicks, can seriously reduce chick survival rates. Whilst commercial fisheries are generally reluctant to curtail activities in the interests of preserving wildlife, in some instances rescheduling of activities can be of enormous benefit to wildlife without being economically damaging.

Reliance on such areas of high productivity varies from species to species. Gentoo Penguins breed in small colonies, rarely exceeding a few hundred pairs in any one colony, and as such exert less competition on the foraging zones around their colony than Rockhoppers, which often nest in huge colonies numbering tens of thousands. In addition, Gentoos are able to move the location of the colony in response to environmental changes, whereas Rockhoppers are committed to remaining at the same breeding sites, whether the foraging zones around those sites are productive or not. Such factors may well help to explain why the Rockhoppers around the Falkland Islands have crashed in numbers over recent years, whilst the Gentoos have not.

Commercial fisheries are not the only threat posed by human activities at sea. It is estimated that 40,000 penguins are killed by oil pollution along the coast of Argentina every year. This oil mostly comes from deliberate operational discharges, such as the emptying of oily ballast water, rather than from accidents. Pollution in Falkland waters has to date been restricted to the occasional oiled bird caught up in small scale spillage from fishing and transport vessels. However now that oil exploration has begun in Falkland waters, there is a real risk that Falkland penguins could become affected in a similar way to those of Argentina.

Because oil tankers are designed to function when fully laden with oil, empty tankers returning to collect another load, must fill the empty tanks with sea water to act as ballast. This oily water should then be discharged at the terminal prior to loading up with fresh oil, in order to prevent oil being discharged into the sea, but this practice is often ignored. Because it is time-consuming to pump the oily water from the tanker at the terminal, the water is often discharged directly into the ocean a few miles before reaching the terminal, in order to make loading faster. The consequences of such malpractice can be devastating to the local wildlife, but enforcing better practices can be almost impossible, even for willing governments.

Oil tankers are governed not by the country whose waters they sail in, but by the country with whom the tanker is registered. Not surprisingly, tankers are often registered under countries which have the most minimal of safety and environmental safeguards, and therefore operate virtually beyond the law. Not only do they continue to discharge oil without fear of prosecution, in order to save money, but often the tankers themselves are poorly maintained, and operated by crews that are untrained in emergency procedures.

Adequate safeguards must be taken to ensure that the highest standards of environmental protection are put in place, to reduce both operational discharges, and to prevent accidents. The problem lies in the fact that governments often claim that they are doing just that, up until the point that an accident proves otherwise. Following major spills around the world, experts often claim to identify the reasons behind the incident, and make changes to regulations to ensure that such accidents cannot happen again. Whilst such measures should be commended, it does allow for complacency to return once more.

It should always be borne in mind that shipping accidents are like car accidents: despite continuous improvements to design and regulations, accidents will inevitably happen. It is therefore essential to have adequate contingency plans to deal with such emergencies, and plans that will be effective in all weather conditions. Most accidents occur in rough weather, and contingency plans must be able to operate under such conditions. It is amazing how many rescue plans cannot be put into operation following a spillage, because they can only be executed in fair weather.

Penguins are amongst the most sensitive of birds to marine oil pollution. Being flightless and having to surface regularly to breath, they are unable to avoid being coated by oil in their vicinity, even when in the open ocean. In addition, because penguins' line of sight is at sea level, they are often unable to see surface oil ahead of them until its too late.

The majority of penguins polluted by operational discharges, are coated in oil out at sea, without the oil ever being noticed on the beaches. Attention is only drawn to the affects of oil pollution when major spills occur, and birds become polluted ashore in large numbers, but in actual fact, the daily mortality of penguins by small scale discharges is far more damaging than a one-off disaster.

Oiled penguins that have been rescued and cleaned, have been shown to have a much higher survival rate than other seabirds. Oil coats the feathers of all birds and breaks down the insulation given by the plumage, however penguins have layers of subcuticular fat which help prevent hypothermia. In addition, penguins are more tolerant of handling than most birds, and are very sociable, which allows them to be housed in large numbers without causing excessive stress. Nevertheless, although cleaning oiled birds can be fairly successful on a small scale, it rarely saves more than a tiny proportion of the victims from a large spill, and can never be considered as a serious proposal for mitigating the damage of large scale oil pollution.

A host of land-based human activities also pose threats to penguin populations, including farming, tourism, industry, poaching, guano removal and introduced predators. Such threats are often specific to certain species, and are therefore discussed separately under each species.

Although all penguin species share many common features, they are also uniquely different from one another. They each occupy different types of coast, and even different regions and climates. They have different lifestyles, have adopted different life strategies, and utilise different resources. Such variations reduce direct competition between species, by allowing them to forage for different sizes or species of prey, and to utilise different nesting sites. These characteristics also give them their individuality, and form the basis of the remaining chapters.

Throughout the book, population sizes are quoted as numbers of breeding pairs. This is the basic unit used for determining breeding populations of birds, for a number of practical reasons. The total number of actual individuals is difficult to determine, since birds often only congregate in order to breed. Even if it were possible to include non-breeding birds, it would not be a very meaningful figure, since it would be subject to too many variables.

In order to make comparisons of population trends, it is important to use a figure which remains as constant as possible in a stable population. Since the number of breeding pairs does not change throughout the year, for example through new chicks or fledgling mortality, it provides a much more useful figure for comparing annual change.

For surface breeding birds which congregate in high density breeding colonies, the locations of these colonies are indicated by spots on the map, with each spot being numbered to correspond to the population data given in the accompanying table. For Magellanic, Humboldt and Galapagos Penguins, which do not congregate in such high density colonies, the breeding distribution is shown by hatching along the areas of coast where colonies may be found.

WEALTH

No virtuous beauty can life bestow,
on men who great starvation know.
But those of wealth should see things true,
that life is more than me and you.

As penguins fish and eagles fly,
does life's mystique not catch your eye?
Without their spectre to behold,
what purpose be to all grow old?

Should cars and TV take the place,
of all we lose of nature's grace?
To crave more wealth than we can spend,
we risk a world we cannot mend.

When oil and penguins both are through,
and children ask us what we do.
Perhaps recall what once we had,
and why we thought is was so bad.

Mike Bingham (May 1996)

PART 2: Diversity of the Species

Dr. Mike Bingham

KING PENGUIN *(Aptenodytes patagonicus)*

Despite the specific name of *patagonicus*, King Penguins no longer breed in Patagonia, or indeed any other part of South America. They used to breed on Islas de los Estados (Staten Island) until the colony was wiped out by sealers in the 19th Century, and moulting adults still come ashore there on occasions. There is a breeding population of about 400 pairs on the Falkland Islands, but this is very small indeed in comparison to the total world population of over one and a half million breeding pairs. The major breeding sites are found on the islands of South Georgia, Crozet, Prince Edward, Kerguelen, Macquarie and Heard, which all lie close to the Antarctic Convergence.

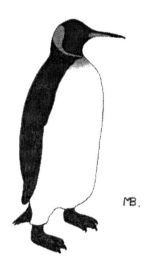

KING PENGUIN

The King Penguin is the largest of the penguins found in the Falklands or South America, with a typical weight of 12 - 14kg, and an average length of 90cm. Length is measured from the tip of the bill to the tip of the tail, in an outstretched bird. This is a more reliable measurement than height, since it is not affected by variations in stance. The King Penguin is second in size only to the Emperor Penguin, which rarely strays far from the frozen waters of the Antarctic.

The King Penguin has distinctive orange patches on each side of the head, which extend down and meet beneath the chin, where they become yellow and fade into the silvery-white breast plumage. The mandibular plates on either side of the bill are also orange in colour. The female is slightly smaller than the male, but has similar plumage.

King Penguins make no nest, and instead lay a single egg of around 310g, which they hold on their feet for the entire incubation period of about 55 days. This adaptation allows breeding in much colder terrain than would be the case for species that lay their eggs on the ground, and negates the need for nesting material. The eggs are brooded by both parents in turn, with shift changes of 6 - 18 days; the non-brooding parent going to sea on extended foraging trips.

The newly hatched chicks are also held on the parents feet for the first 30 - 40 days, by which time they have developed their mesoptile plumage, and are able to regulate their own body temperature. During chick-rearing, parents continue to take turns at brooding, but change over periods vary from 3 - 14 days, so chicks may have fairly prolonged waits between feeds. The King Penguin is known to travel far from the Falkland Islands in search of food during chick-rearing.

Chicks are eventually left in creches, to allow both adults to go to sea on prolonged foraging trips, with chicks being fed even less frequently. During the austral winter chicks may go for periods of up to 3 months between feeds, and healthy chicks have been shown to be able to survive for up to 5 months without a feed. It is quite common for chicks to lose 50% of their body weight whilst waiting for food.

Despite this lack of food, King Penguin chicks are still able to survive prolonged periods of extremely cold weather. This is achieved by increasing metabolic activity through the burning of body fat in muscle tissue, despite remaining inactive. Stored body fat reserves are usually adequate to maintain the chicks for at least 3 months, but as body fat reserves become depleted, chicks must begin to break down body protein to provide energy. Weight loss then becomes more rapid, and starvation would eventually result unless the chick was fed. Nevertheless, starvation does not usually result until a chick, which perhaps weighed around 10kg at the start of winter, has gone down to just 3kg. Very few animals are able to survive a 70% loss of body weight, and still be capable of recovery.

Preferred breeding sites are flat coastal plains within easy reach of the ocean via a sandy beach. The breeding cycle is different to that of other Falkland penguins, with chicks taking the better part of a year to fledge. This requires them to overwinter at the breeding colony, and during this period the chicks remain in creches, and are well insulated from the cold by their long brown downy coats. They eventually fledge the following summer, and will not return to breed until they are at least 3 years of age.

King Penguins can live to over 30 years of age in captivity, and in the wild they normally return to the same site to breed throughout their life. Breeding is preceded by the annual moult, which lasts 4 to 5 weeks. Their return to the breeding colony is poorly synchronised, and hence birds often change partners each breeding cycle.

A complete breeding cycle lasts over a year. This tends to result in individual birds having their following breeding cycle out of phase with other birds, thus large chicks and eggs may both occur in a colony at the same time. Because the Falklands population is so small, at several sites there are insufficient breeding birds to form a colony. When adult numbers drop below about 15 individuals, they tend to merge with Gentoo Penguin colonies. This presumably offers some of the benefits of colony life, such as greater protection from predators, but because Gentoo chicks fledge by February, King Penguin chicks are left to overwinter alone.

King Penguins are remarkably curious of humans, and the chicks in particular will approach to investigate people who are sitting quietly, using their bills to probe boot laces, hair, or anything else that takes their fancy. By contrast the adults can be quite aggressive towards each other in the colony, pecking and beating each other with their flippers. Adults announce themselves by extending the neck to look skywards and giving out a trumpet like call. The chicks by comparison usher a squeaky piping call.

King Penguins generally forage at depths of 150 - 300m, with 300m being around the maximum depth recorded for this species. These are the deepest dives of any penguin, except for the Emperor Penguin which is not found outside the frozen waters of Antarctica. King Penguins mainly feed on small bioluminous Lanternfish, and some squid, (including *Gonatus antarcticus, Onychoteuthis sp.* and *Moroteuthis sp.*). Deep dives are only made during the daytime, but King Penguins can also feed at night by making shallow dives. Presumably they can still hunt by sight at night because of the bioluminous light emitted from their prey. Since light penetration does not appear to be the only factor determining foraging depth, it could be that foraging depth is largely determined by diurnal migration of prey species in response to day and night. In the Falkland Islands the foraging range extends to the edge of the Antarctic Peninsula, to the Atlantic coast of South America as far north as Buenos Aires, and across to South Georgia and perhaps beyond.

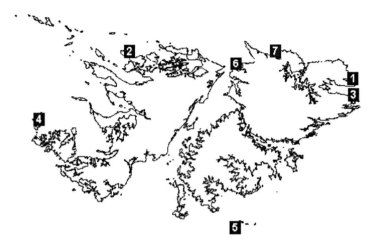

Map of King Penguin colonies in the Falkland Islands

A complete census of all breeding sites during the 1995/96 breeding season, recorded a total of 339 chicks for the Falklands as a whole. Allowing for losses during incubation and chick-rearing, and the staggered breeding cycle, this figure gives an estimated Falklands population of around 400 breeding pairs. Volunteer Point was confirmed as the only major breeding site for King Penguins in the Falklands. This colony has expanded from 38 chicks in 1980/81 to 330 chicks in 1995/96. Nevertheless the Falklands' population still comprises less than 0.03% of the world population, and its high rate of increase over the last 10 or 15 years is likely to be due in part to immigration from the rapidly expanding population on South Georgia.

King Penguins at Volunteer Point are often preyed upon by Orcas (Killer Whales), which patrol close to shore in search of Gentoo, Magellanic and King Penguins. Sea Lions and Leopard Seals also take penguins around Falkland waters. There are no terrestrial predators which pose a threat to adult King Penguins, but birds such as skuas and gulls will take eggs and small chicks if they get the opportunity. This is particularly the case when just

27

one or two pairs of King Penguin breed in a Gentoo colony, since the King Penguin chicks lack the protection of a creche when the Gentoo chicks leave in February.

Human impact is currently very low, despite King Penguins being a great tourist attraction. They are very tolerant of human presence, and are not alarmed by the presence of tourists provided that they remain at the outskirts of the colony. There is no direct exploitation of King Penguins in the Falkland Islands, and they are seldom caught as a result of commercial fishing, other than through the occasional discarded net. There is very little overlap between the prey of King Penguin, and the commercially harvested species of squid and fish. The Falklands fishing industry is therefore unlikely to greatly influence King Penguin population trends. By contrast, the fact that virtually the entire Falklands' population exists at one location, makes it very susceptible to an incident such as an oil spill in that vicinity.

GENTOO PENGUIN (*Pygoscelis papua*)

The Gentoo Penguin is numerous and widespread in the Falkland Islands, but has only one very tiny breeding colony in South America, on Islas de los Estados. World-wide there are about 320,000 breeding pairs of Gentoo, and a census conducted by the author during 1995/96, shows that the Falkland Islands hold the second largest population with 65,000 pairs. Other populations are found on the Antarctic Peninsula, and the islands of South Georgia, Kerguelen, Heard, South Orkney, Macquarie, Crozet, Prince Edward and South Sandwich.

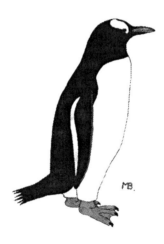

GENTOO PENGUIN

Gentoos are the second largest Falkland penguin, with an average length of 80cm and an average weight of 5kg. They have a reddish orange bill, apart from the black culminicorn, and orange feet. White patches above each eye meet across the crown, with white speckling in the adjacent black plumage around the head. Females are slightly smaller than the males, but have similar markings.

Breeding colonies are scattered throughout the Falklands, and rarely consist of more than a few hundred breeding pairs. When colonies exceed this size, they break up into smaller subcolonies adjacent to each other. The preferred nesting sites are low coastal plains, fairly close to a sandy or shingle beach, which is used to gain access to the open ocean. A substantial amount of guano and waste accumulates around the nesting area during the breeding season, and colonies usually move a short distance onto fresh ground each season, retaining the same path to the sea.

Gentoos are ground nesting birds, making rudimentary nests from stones, sticks, grass, feathers, or practically any material that they can find suitable for the purpose. Egg-laying is usually completed by late October, with two equally sized eggs of about 130g being laid. Incubation takes about 34 days, with both parents sharing incubation duties, and nest changes occurring every 1 - 3 days. Despite the two eggs being laid 4 days apart from each other, they both hatch within the space of 24 hours.

The female's reproductive tract actually produces three eggs, and she can lay these at 4 day intervals, however the third egg is only laid if she loses her first two eggs. This enables the third egg to be laid within just 4 days of losing the first eggs, and if it is not needed, the third egg is re-absorbed into the body. Even if the third egg is also lost, the female can still produce a completely new clutch of eggs within a month. This is a truly remarkable adaptation to egg-loss from avian predators, and helps to explain the folklore that Gentoos fare better when colonies have the first eggs removed.

The young chicks remain in the nest until they grow their mesoptile plumage at about 3 - 4 weeks of age. During this period both parents brood the chicks alternately, feeding the chicks and changing over on a daily basis. Adults usually set out to forage in the early morning, returning later the same day, and foraging generally occurs within 20km of the breeding site. The time spent foraging increases as chicks get larger, and their demand for food gets greater.

After the brood period, chicks are able to leave the nest and form into large creches, allowing both parents to collect food to meet the ever increasing demand. The mesoptile plumage has similar markings to the adult plumage, except that the dark areas are a browny grey rather than black, and there is no white head patch.

Gentoos put equal effort into raising both chicks, and have the ability to produce large numbers of chicks in seasons of high food availability. During such seasons of plenty, even deformed chicks which are unable to walk properly, may be reared to the point of fledging. By contrast, when food is scarce there is strong competition for food between chicks, and only the strongest survive. Adults are often observed running through the colony, closely pursued by one or two hungry chicks. This may well be part of the selection procedure, whereby the strongest, hungriest or most determined chick gets fed.

Chicks fledge at around 14 weeks of age, but may continue to be fed by the parents for several weeks after fledging. After completion of the breeding season, adults spend time at sea building up body fat reserves prior to undergoing their annual moult. The moult takes around 2 to 3 weeks, and during this time birds spend considerable amounts of time tending to their plumage. Gentoos do not allopreen.

Gentoo populations are characterised by large annual fluctuations in population size and breeding success, with the later ranging between 0.5 and 1.5 chicks fledged per breeding pair. Gentoos are capable of breeding at just 2 years of age.

Because Gentoos at most sites tend to move the colony a few metres each year, they do not retain the same nests from year to year. On occasions whole colonies that have remained at one site for years, will up and move to a new site many kilometres away, for no apparent reason. This may happen suddenly during a single year, or gradually over a number of years.

By comparison with other penguins, Gentoo pair-bonds are often long-lasting, despite annual nest changes. Many adults remain around the colony throughout the year, whilst others take the opportunity during the winter months to make longer foraging trips further afield.

Gentoos generally forage close to shore at depths of 20 - 100m, although they have been recorded diving to depths of more than 200m. Gentoos may make as many as 450 dives during a single days foraging. Penguins all look clumsy on land, but in fact the Gentoo can out-run a man over short distances, and often situates its colony 1 or 2 kilometres from the sea.

Gentoos are opportunistic feeders, and around the Falklands are known to take roughly equal proportions of fish (such as *Patagonotothen sp., Thysanopsetta naresi* and *Micromesistius australis*), lobster krill (*Munida gregaria*) and squid (especially *Loligo gahi, Gonatus antarcticus* and *Moroteuthis ingens*).

A complete census of Gentoo Penguins conducted during the 1995/96 season, showed that they breed at 81 sites throughout the Falkland Islands, and have a total population of around 65,000 breeding pairs. Breeding populations at these 81 sites ranged from 7 to 5100 breeding pairs, but sites of more than a few hundred pairs consisted of several subcolonies. The general distribution was:

East Falkland - 16,000 pairs   **West Falkland** - 24,000 pairs
Outer Islands - 25,000 pairs   **FI TOTAL** - **65,000 pairs**

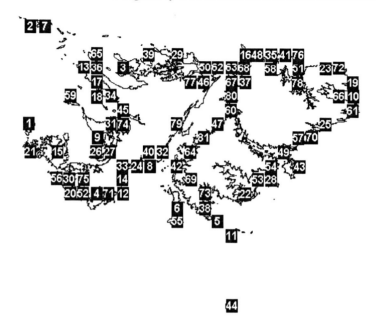

Map of Gentoo breeding sites in the Falkland Islands

Research by the author shows that Gentoo Penguin numbers declined in the Falklands during the 1980's and into the 1990's, but this was against the general trend for Gentoo populations world-wide.

At sea, Gentoos are subject to predation by Sea Lions, Leopard Seals and Orcas. On occasions Sea Lions have been known to come inland after penguins, and even Fur Seals can disrupt breeding colonies on occasions. Nevertheless such incidents are rare, and Gentoo colonies are usually placed far enough inland to avoid such threats.

On land healthy adults have no natural predators, but skuas, gulls and birds of prey, such as caracaras, will steal eggs and small chicks if they get the opportunity. Chicks are also at risk from fluctuations in food supply and weather. Mesoptile plumage provides good insulation when dry, but if it becomes saturated by prolonged rain, chicks can die from hypothermia. By contrast in periods of very hot weather, chicks become too hot, and may die from heat stress.

Although human activity has greatly modified the landscape around the Falklands, Gentoo Penguins prefer open plains to breed, and consequently have not been greatly affected by the loss of the tall tussac grass. Gentoos are also very tolerant of grazing animals, such as sheep, cattle and horses, which often wander around Gentoo colonies without causing alarm.

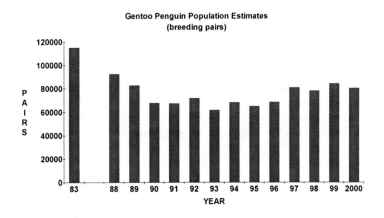

Gentoo Penguin Population Estimates (breeding pairs)

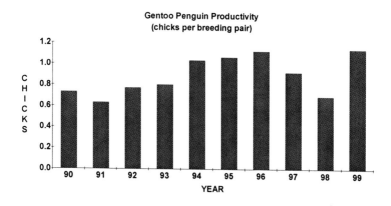

The expansion of roads throughout the Falklands, along with the increase in resident population and tourism, has greatly increased the level of disturbance at many Gentoo colonies. Nevertheless, studies of population numbers and breeding success show no evidence that Gentoos are at risk from current levels of disturbance. Gentoos become tolerant of human presence, and do not generally become alarmed unless people approach within about 15m of the nest site.

For many years the rural communities of the Falkland Islands took Gentoo eggs for food. Until recent years these eggs were an important supplement to the diet of many folk, but now with regular supplies of hen eggs the tradition is gradually dying out. Penguin eggs are always taken at the start of incubation, and the birds rapidly re-lay, so that colonies which have had eggs taken show little difference in productivity by the time chicks are ready to fledge. This observation, along with the way that Gentoo colonies fluctuate in size without apparent cause, has led to much speculation about the merits of egging.

Many landowners believe that hatching rates are higher for the second brood, because a higher proportion of first brood eggs are infertile, but there is no scientific evidence to support this theory. Another theory is that because all the first brood eggs are removed at the same time, the second brood is more evenly aged than the first, which makes it more difficult for skuas and gulls to pick on smaller, weaker members of the colony. In addition the later brooding puts the colony out of phase with the needs of the predators, which are denied their food source at the start of their brooding period.

This second theory is harder to evaluate, and there could be some merit in it. On balance however, after much study of sites which are egged and those which are not, there is no obvious difference in chick rearing success rates either way, and this centuries old tradition probably has little impact one way or the other, provided it is not abused.

Human impact at sea is more difficult to evaluate. There is considerable commercial fishing activity in Falklands waters for squid and finfish. Diet analysis shows that there is considerable overlap between those species being commercially harvested, and those which make up the diet of Gentoo Penguins. Whilst it is true to say that the Falklands fisheries industry is well managed by international standards, the main aim of this management is to ensure that stocks are not over exploited commercially, rather than to consider the effects on wildlife.

Food abundance does not so much control penguin populations through the occasional mass starvation, but rather through subtle changes in how effectively penguins are able to raise chicks, survive into adulthood and breed into old age. Any reduction in the abundance of prey will effect the ability of penguins to gather enough food to live and breed.

Life for a penguin is a constant balance between the energy expended hunting for food, and the energy gained by the food caught. Even a small reduction in food abundance means that penguins spend longer, and use more energy, searching for prey. This balance becomes critical during the early stages of chick rearing, when just one adult from each pair can feed at any given time, and yet food is required by both adults and growing chicks. The situation is further complicated by the fact that the foraging range is restricted to how far each penguin can travel in a single day. During chick-rearing Gentoos rely on feeding areas within 20km of their nest-site.

The Falkland Islands are internationally important as both commercial fishing grounds and seabird breeding sites for essentially the same reason; the richness of the marine food resource. Prior to any commercial fishing activity, seabird and marine mammal population sizes would have been largely controlled by food abundance. Within the overall ecosystem, there would have been many interacting cycles of predator-prey relationships, but all these food chains would have depended on the overall food availability. Any reduction in this level of food availability, be it from natural or human factors, will inevitably lead to a reduction of the populations which it can support.

Direct mortality from human activities has generally been low. Few penguins are caught by fishing vessels, other than through discarded nets and marine refuse. There had also been very little pollution around Falklands waters until 1998, when oil exploration led to three separate oil spills that killed several hundred penguins.

SOUTHERN ROCKHOPPER (*Eudyptes c. chrysocome*)

World-wide there are 3 subspecies of Rockhopper Penguin; Southern Rockhopper being the name given to the subspecies *Eudyptes chrysocome chrysocome,* which is restricted to the Falkland Islands and South America. Censuses conducted by the author during 1995/96 and 1996/97 show that the Falkland Islands hold about two thirds of the population with 300,000 breeding pairs, and South America the remaining one third with about 175,000 pairs. South Georgia is also known to hold a few breeding pairs, but only around 10 pairs have been recorded.

ROCKHOPPER PENGUIN

Rockhoppers are amongst the smallest of the world's penguins, having an average length of around 52cm, and an average weight of about 3kg. A yellow stripe above each eye projects into a yellow crest, and these are joined behind the head by a black occipital crest. The eyes are red, the short bulbous bill is reddish brown, and the feet and legs are pink. The Southern Rockhopper is distinguished from other Rockhoppers by having black skin around the bill, and a shorter occipital crest. The females are slightly smaller than the males, but have similar plumage.

Rockhopper breeding colonies may be very large; up to a hundred thousand nests may be present at a single breeding site. Nesting densities range from 1.5 to 3 nests per sq.m., and colonies are often shared with nesting albatross or cormorants. Rockhoppers return not only to the same breeding site each year, but also utilise the same nest, which they refurbish with stones, sticks, vegetation or any other suitable material.

The preferred nesting sites are steep rocky gullies, above approaches into deep water. Such sites may be vegetated by grasses or dwarf shrubs, but long-established colonies will generally have destroyed most of the natural vegetation surrounding the colony, and worn a pathway from the sea up the rockface. Rockhoppers regularly bathe and drink fresh water, and most breeding sites are close to natural springs or freshwater puddles.

The breeding cycle begins in early October, with males arriving at the breeding site a few days earlier than the females. Copulation begins as soon as the females arrive, and egg-laying takes place in early November. Two eggs are laid 4 - 5 days apart, with the first egg hatching later than the second. The first egg, at around 80g, is considerably smaller than the second egg of around 110g. This strategy aims to rear just one healthy chick under a wide range of circumstances. The second egg is generally brooded at the rear, where the temperature is more stable, and where it is less prone to being lost or stolen.

In other subspecies of Rockhopper it is almost unheard of for both chicks to ever be reared, but the Southern Rockhopper is capable of rearing both chicks to fledging when conditions are favourable. Even so, Southern Rockhoppers have low annual fluctuations in population size and chick rearing success, and annual productivity never exceeds 1 chick fledged per breeding pair.

Incubation of the eggs takes around 33 days, and is divided into three roughly equal shifts. During the first shift both parents are in attendance. The male then goes to sea to feed while the female takes the second shift, and he returns to relieve the female for the third shift. The male remains on the nest until the eggs hatch, and continues to brood the chicks for the first 25 days, while the female brings food for the chicks.

Such a system of extended shift duration requires lengthy fasts for both parents, but allows them to forage further afield than would be the case if they had a daily change-over. The newly hatched chicks may have to wait for up to a week before the female returns with their first feed. During this period chicks are able to survive on existing yolk reserves, after which they begin receiving regular feeds of around 150g in weight.

By the end of the 25 days of brooding, chicks have developed their mesoptile plumage, and are receiving regular feeds averaging around 600g. By this stage they are able to leave the nest and creche with other chicks, allowing both adults to forage to meet the chicks' increasing demands for food. Rockhopper creches are not generally as large as those of Gentoo Penguins, possibly due to the more rugged terrain, and the chicks creche into numerous small groups scattered throughout the colony.

Chicks completely lack the yellow markings of the adult birds, and even the bills are black. As chicks moult into adult plumage, the colony is joined by pre-breeding birds arriving to moult. These birds are distinguished from newly fledged chicks by a faint yellow stripe above the eye, and a reddish brown bill. The crest is not developed until birds mature. Rockhoppers do not breed until at least 4 years of age, but have been shown to live for up to 25 years in captivity.

Despite being the smallest of the penguins found in the Falklands or South America, they are perhaps the most aggressive. They show little fear of people, or of birds and animals larger than themselves. Anything that comes within range of an incubating bird will be pecked, including any other Rockhopper, or the long wings of neighbouring albatross. This is perhaps one reason why King Cormorants (*Phalacrocorax atriceps*) prefer to nest amongst Rockhoppers, benefiting from the latter's aggression towards potential predators that might try to steal eggs or small chicks. Nevertheless, Rockhoppers can be very gentle with their partners, and allopreening is common.

Chicks fledge at around 10 weeks of age, and adults then spend 20 - 25 days at sea building up subcuticular body fat reserves in preparation for their annual moult. The moult lasts for around 25 days, and the birds then abandon the breeding site and spend the winter feeding at sea, prior to returning the following spring.

Rockhoppers are opportunistic feeders, and around the Falklands are known to take varying proportions of crustaceans (*Euphausia lucens, E. vallentini, Thysanoessa gregaria* and *Themisto sp.*), squid (*Gonatus antarcticus, Loligo gahi, Onychoteuthis sp,* and *Teuthowenia sp.*) and various small fish. Foraging dives rarely exceed 100m depth, but feeding in groups is common.

A complete census of Southern Rockhopper penguins was conducted by the author during 1995 (Falklands) and 1996 (South America). These censuses recorded a total of 297,000 breeding pairs at 36 sites in the Falkland Islands, and 175,000 breeding pairs at 15 sites in South America, giving a world total of 472,000 pairs.

In 1984 the Falklands population had been estimated at 2,500,000 pairs, so the 1995 Falklands census revealed a massive 88% decline in just 11 years. What is more, nearby populations in South America had shown no signs of decline during this period, the decline was unique to the Falklands.

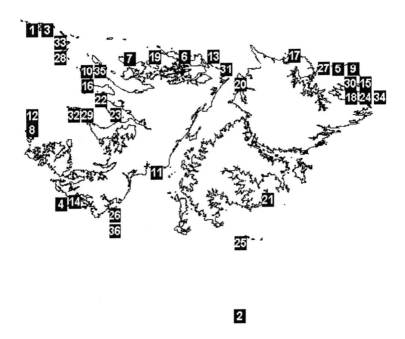

Map of Rockhopper breeding sites in the Falkland Islands

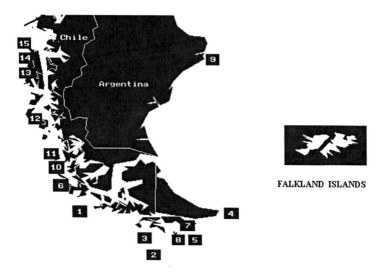

FALKLAND ISLANDS

Map of Rockhopper breeding sites in South America

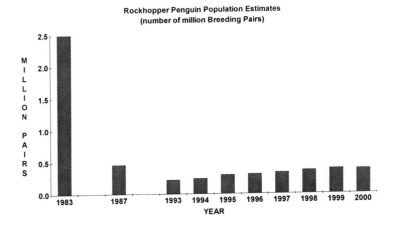

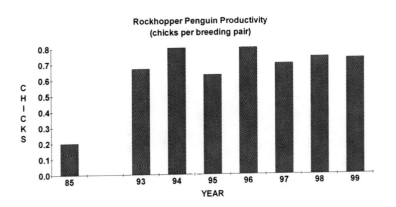

Population declines in the Falklands were greatest during the 1980's and early 1990's, when commercial fishing activity was at its height. During the 1980s the situation became so severe that adult Rockhoppers were unable to find sufficient food to build up body fat reserves, and hundreds of thousands starved to death during their annual, with Falklands breeding sites becoming littered with bodies.

Following the discovery of this dramatic decline (see Preface), fishing effort in Falklands waters has been reduced, and Rockhopper penguin populations have begun to recover. By the year 2000, Falklands Rockhopper populations had recovered to around 400,000 breeding pairs, and now seem to be in balance with the level of food available under the current fishing regime. Nevertheless, whilst commercial fishing continues, it is unlikely that populations will ever return to the 2,500,000 breeding pairs recorded in 1984.

Evidence of this massive decline can be seen from the breeding sites themselves. Falkland Islands colonies are all old colonies, where the ground has generally been cleared of vegetation by years of occupation. At most sites, a pocket of nests now lie at the centre of an area cleared by a colony that was once much larger. By contrast, breeding sites in Chile and Argentina contain new, middle-aged and old colonies, indicating a natural cycle of fluctuation and regeneration. In particular, populations on Isla de los Estados (Staten Island) and Isla Noir are known to be expanding into areas of dense vegetation.

Healthy adults do not have any predators on land, although skuas, gulls and caracaras will take eggs and young. Predators such as Sea Lions and Orcas take Rockhoppers at sea, indeed it is not unheard of for Sea Lions to come into Rockhopper breeding sites that are too close to the sea, but such natural predation cannot explain the Rockhoppers decline. In actual fact their main predator, the Southern Sea Lion, has declined in the Falklands at a greater rate than the Rockhopper, with populations now standing at just 1% of their former size.

The mass starvation of Falklands penguins in 1985 marked the end of unregulated commercial fishing in Falklands waters. A government Fisheries Department was subsequently established to license and regulate what had become a free for all. Since regulations have been in place, fishing effort has gradually been reduced, and there have been no further mass mortalities of penguins. Since the mid 1990s an improvement in breeding success has been observed, with annual productivity now ranging from 0.6 to 0.9 chicks fledged per breeding pair. This improvement in breeding success brought an end to population declines, and populations now appear to be stable.

Even so, the level of fishing activity around Rockhopper breeding sites in South America is still very much lower than that found around the Falkland Islands. It is possible that part of the Falklands decline may have been the result of migration to Isla de los Estados (Staten Island) in Argentina, where populations have increased dramatically over recent years.

The harvesting of eggs from Rockhopper Penguin colonies is no longer permitted in the Falkland Islands. Nevertheless, egging is still carried out on a large scale by avian predators. Rockhoppers do not possess the same ability to re-lay as Gentoo Penguins.

With the entire world population of Southern Rockhoppers being restricted to the Falkland Islands and southern South America, serious measures need to be considered in order to ensure that human activities do not further reduce population size. Even so, Rockhoppers are very tolerant of human presence if care is taken. In the Falkland Islands, Rockhopper Penguins are a major tourist attraction, and a number of sites have large numbers of visitors every year.

Comparison of sites which have large numbers of visitors, with those that have none, show no differences in breeding success or population trends. Rockhoppers have no fear of people, treating all invaders into their space with the same aggression as that shown to a trespassing neighbour. Provided that visitors do not try entering the colony, breeding birds will generally carry on with their business as usual, and a calm approach to within about 5m of the colony is likely to leave one surrounded by inquisitive birds. This tolerance provides an excellent opportunity for a sustainable tourist industry, which could give added incentive to safeguarding future populations for more than just their intrinsic value.

At the recent international workshop reviewing the status of penguins, it was clear that the large scale declines in Rockhopper Penguin populations were of such magnitude as to justify treating the species as globally threatened (Vulnerable), according to the new IUCN criteria.

MACARONI PENGUIN *(Eudyptes chrysolophus)*

The Macaroni Penguin is the most numerous of all the world's penguins, with an estimated world population of over 9 million breeding pairs. The main breeding sites are found on the islands of South Georgia, Crozet, Kerguelen, Heard, McDonald, Prince Edward and Bouvetoya, with other notable colonies in the South Shetlands, South Orkneys and islands off the coast of Southern Chile. The Falkland Islands has a population which averages less than 50 breeding pairs, whilst the South American population stands at around 12,000 breeding pairs.

MACARONI PENGUIN

Macaronis are substantially larger than Rockhoppers, having an average length of around 70cm and an average weight of 5.5kg. They are the largest members of the genus *Eudyptes*. The head and upperparts are bluish black, and the underparts are white. The large reddish brown bill has exposed pink skin at its base; the eyes are red and the legs and feet are pink. The most distinctive features are the golden yellow crests which extend from the centre of the forehead and sweep backwards above the eyes. Females are smaller than the males, but have similar plumage. Juveniles lack the elegant crests, and have dull brown eyes, and browny black bills.

In South America there are nine sites with Macaroni breeding colonies, but only the islands of Diego Ramirez, Ildefonso and Noir hold more than a thousand breeding pairs. There are no Macaroni breeding colonies in the Falklands, due to the population being too small. Instead Macaronis may be found breeding individually amongst Rockhoppers in any of the Rockhopper colonies. Macaronis begin breeding about two weeks later than Rockhoppers, but choose similar sites on rocky coasts and low cliffs. Nesting densities range from 0.7 to 1.4 nests per sq.m.

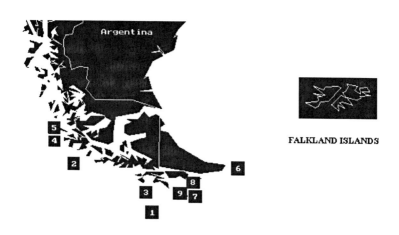

FALKLAND ISLANDS

Map of Macaroni Penguin breeding sites in South America

Two eggs are laid with a period of 4 - 5 days between the two. The first egg weighs about 93g and the second egg about

150g. The first egg is not only considerably smaller, but takes longer to incubate, and is rarely successful. Studies have shown that the first egg is often lost prior to the laying of the second egg, making it of little value as a backup. If both eggs are lost Macaronis do not re-lay.

Incubation takes about 5 weeks, and incubation duties are divided into three roughly equal shifts. Both parents remain at the nest for the first shift, after which the male goes to sea, and the female remains to do the second shift alone. When the male returns to do the third shift, the female goes to sea and does not return until the chicks have hatched. Regardless of the time spent at sea during incubation, Macaronis always come ashore during daylight. On occasions the chick may have to wait for up to a week after hatching to receive its first feed. Meal sizes for the chicks average around 200g at this stage.

The male continues to brood the chick for the first 24 days, while the female collects food for the chick. The chicks are fed on a daily basis, with the females leaving the colony in early morning, and returning with food later the same day. The time spent foraging increases as the chicks get larger, and they require more food to maintain their growth. Macaronis rarely forage more than 40km from the nest site during early chick-rearing.

By the end of the 24 days, the chicks have developed their mesoptile plumage, with dark grey upperparts and creamy white underparts. The mesoptile plumage, along with internal physiological changes, allows the chick to maintain its own body temperature away from the nest, and both parents are then able to forage at sea. This is important, since chick meal sizes can now be up to around 1000g per feed. When both parents are away at sea, the chicks gather into creches in order to gain protection from predators and cold weather.

Chicks develop their waterproof plumage and fledge at about 11 weeks of age. They still lack the crests of the adults, and have instead a scattering of small yellow feathers. They also differ in having blackish brown bills and brown eyes. Once the chicks have left, the adults spend a period of about three weeks at sea feeding in preparation for their annual moult. The moult lasts about 25 days, and adults then leave the breeding sites completely, and spend the winter months at sea.

Females can begin breeding at 5 years of age, but the males do not normally breed until at least 6 years old. This may be a consequence of there being a greater number of males than females, allowing females to select more experienced males as partners. By contrast females can usually find a partner from amongst the surplus of males, as soon as they are physically able to attempt breeding. During their breeding life Macaronis show high site and mate fidelity.

Macaroni's feed on various crustaceans (*Euphausia sp., Thysanoessa sp., Munida gregaria* and *Themisto gaudichaudii)*, squid *(Loligo gahi, Gonatus antarcticus*) and fish *(Notothenia sp.,* and *Champsocephalus gunneri).* During chick-rearing, foraging for food is generally conducted on a daily basis, with adults returning to the nest site before dark. Macaronis normally forage at depths of 15 - 70m, but have been recorded diving down to 100m on occasions. Some night foraging does occur, but dives are much shallower, ranging from only 3 - 6m depth. Dives rarely exceed 2 minutes in duration at any time.

The South American and Falkland populations of Macaroni Penguins are very small in comparison to the world total, and are found in remote areas where human impact on land is minimal. Natural predators such as Sea Lions and Orcas take adult Macaronis at sea, whilst gulls, skuas and birds of prey patrol breeding sites for eggs and young. With current populations being so high, there are no special concerns over current trends.

Dr. Mike Bingham

MAGELLANIC PENGUIN *(Spheniscus magellanicus)*

The Magellanic Penguin is only found around the Falkland Islands and South America, but is extremely numerous within these regions. It is found throughout the Falkland Islands, which hold a total breeding population of over 100,000 breeding pairs. The South American population numbers around one and a half million breeding pairs, with 650,000 pairs breeding along the Atlantic coast of Argentina alone. Breeding colonies range from the Golfo San Matías in Argentina, southwards around the islands of Tierra del Fuego, and northwards up the Pacific coast of Chile as far north as Coquimbo.

MAGELLANIC PENGUIN

The Magellanic Penguin is around 70cm long, and has an average weight of about 4kg. The head and upper parts are black apart from two broad white stripes beneath the throat; one running up behind the cheeks and above the eye to join the pinkish gape, the second running adjacent to the white underparts with which they merge above the legs. Females are slightly smaller than the males, but have similar plumage.

Penguins of the Genus *Spheniscus*, to which Magellanic, Humboldt and Galapagos Penguins all belong, are much more loosely colonial than other penguins. They generally nest in burrows when soil conditions permit, and are consequently spaced much further apart than surface-nesting penguins. Magellanic Penguin colonies in particular often extend over several kilometres of coastline, at densities ranging from 0.001 to 0.1 nests per sq.m.

Magellanic Penguins are widely distributed throughout the Falklands, both on the mainlands and on offshore islands. They particularly like islands with tussac grass, and even very small tussac islands may hold colonies of Magellanic Penguins. The numerous offshore islands around Tierra del Fuego and the Pacific coast of Chile also offer similar nesting habitat. By contrast, the mainlands of East and West Falkland generally have very little remaining tussac grass as a result of livestock grazing, but Magellanic Penguins also nest on these coastal plains. These breeding sites have more in common with many of the mainland colonies of Argentina, where livestock has also altered the natural vegetation.

Magellanic Penguins excavate burrows in any suitable soil type, and when conditions do not favour burrowing they will nest on the surface in shallow depressions, cracks in rocks or under bushes. Adults arrive at the nest sites to breed in September, and after a period of burrow excavation and repair, begin egg laying around mid October. Two equally sized eggs are laid 4 days apart, each with a weight of around 125g.

Incubation takes around 40 days, with the female incubating the eggs for the first shift, while the male feeds at sea. He forages at distances of up to 500km away from the breeding site, before returning to relieve the female some 15 or 20 days later.

She then goes to sea for a similar period, and when she returns, the two birds change over at regular intervals until the eggs hatch.

Both parents continue to brood the chicks in turn, on a daily basis, for a period of about 30 days. The chicks are generally fed on a daily basis, with adults leaving the colony in early morning, and returning with food later the same day. Magellanic Penguins mostly forage within about 40km from the nest site during this period. The foraging trips become longer as the chicks become larger, and demand more food, and chicks may then have to wait several days between meals.

By the end of 30 days the chicks have developed their mesoptile plumage, and are able to venture out of the burrows. At this stage they look very different from the adults, being a browny grey above, and creamy white below. Living in burrows, chicks have good protection from both predators and cold weather while both parents are away feeding, and consequently they do not form creches in the way that most surface-breeding species do.

Whilst burrows offer good protection from most weather conditions, heavy rain can result in flooding of the burrows in certain areas. Chicks rarely drown in such circumstances, but often become wet and cold. Mesoptile plumage provides excellent insulation when dry, but it lacks the waterproofing qualities of the adult plumage and loses much of its insulation properties when wet. Consequently many chicks can die from hypothermia in such conditions. Living in burrows also means that both chicks and adults become infested with penguin fleas.

Despite the two eggs being of roughly equal size, adults give feeding priority to the first chick to hatch, resulting in a higher rate of mortality amongst second chicks. Nevertheless Magellanic Penguins often rear two chicks successfully when sufficient food can be caught. Normal productivity ranges from 0.8 to 1.6 chicks fledged per breeding pair, depending on conditions. Magellanic Penguins do not normally relay if they loose their clutch.

When the weather is fine larger chicks often sit outside their burrow entrances, but will rapidly return to the safety of their burrows at the first sign of danger. Fledging occurs at 9 to 17 weeks of age, depending on food. Fledglings look similar to the adults, except for being greyer and lacking the clearly defined banding of the adults.

Freedom from parental responsibilities allows the adults to spend a period of time at sea, feeding up in preparation for their annual moult in March. Moulting takes 3 to 4 weeks, after which the adults leave the breeding site, and remain at sea until the following breeding season. Magellanic Penguins can live to about 20 years of age.

Females may begin breeding at 4 years of age, but the males do not normally breed until they are at least 5 years old. This is quite possibly a consequence of there being more males than females, making it easier for inexperienced females to find partners than for inexperienced males. Magellanic penguins generally show strong site and mate fidelity, and pair-bonds are reinforced by allopreening.

Magellanic penguins are opportunistic feeders, taking roughly equal proportions of fish (such as *Micromesistius australis, Sprattus fuegensis, Engraulis anchoita, Merluccius hubbsi, Patagonotothen sp., Austroatherina sp.* and *Myxinus sp.*), squid (*Loligo gahi, Gonatus antarcticus, Moroteuthis ingens* and *Onychoteuthis sp.*) and lobster krill (*Munida gregaria*). During chick-rearing, foraging trips are generally conducted on a daily basis during daylight hours, except in the Falklands where food is harder to find. Birds generally forage at depths of less than 50m, but on occasions may dive up to 100m. Winter foraging for prey often takes them way beyond their normal breeding range, with birds travelling as far north as Brazil.

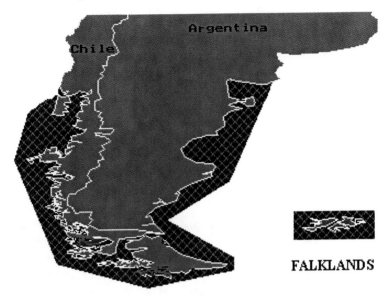

Map showing world distribution of Magellanic Penguins

Magellanic Penguins declined severely in the Falkland Islands during the 1980's and 1990's, which coincided with the rise of commercial fishing for squid and finfish. The current Falklands population (2000) stands at less than 30% of its 1988 level, and this decline is still continuing. These declines have not occurred in nearby Chile.

Comparisons of colonies in the Falklands and Chile appear to confirm that competition with commercial fishing is a major cause of the Falklands decline. Adult penguins in Chile are able to return with food to their chicks on a daily basis, with foraging trips averaging 16 to 18 hours. By contrast adults in the Falkland Islands take approximately 35 hours to find the same amount of food.

With only half the amount of food being fed to chicks, lower chick survival rates would be expected, and this is confirmed by our research. Over recent years breeding success and chick survival rates have been substantially higher in Chile (average

1.35 chicks per nest) than in the Falklands (average 0.82 chicks per nest). This huge difference in breeding success is sufficient to account for the gradual decline in population, with insufficient chicks being reared in the Falklands to replace natural adult mortality.

On Isla Magdalena in Chile, which is only 600km from the Falklands, only 24% of breeding adults fail to raise at least one chick. In the Falklands however, this is an incredible 63%. Almost two-thirds of all nests completely fail in the Falklands, and of those that do survive, only 21% raise two chicks, compared to 45% on Isla Magdalena. Isla Magdalena lies in the Straits of Magellan where commercial fishing is prohibited on environmental grounds.

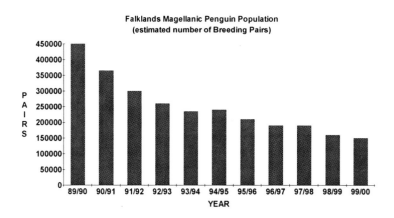

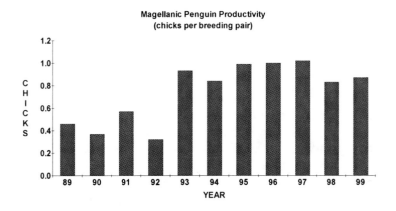

Magellanic Penguin Productivity
(chicks per breeding pair)

The breeding sites themselves also show the magnitude of the Falklands decline. In the Falklands, populations have declined so much that 80 to 90% of burrows are unoccupied or derelict. A Magellanic Penguin in the Falkland Islands has no difficulty finding a suitable burrow. There are plenty of ready made ones whose owners have either died or moved elsewhere. On Isla Magdalena, virtual every inch is used by penguins. Even areas where the ground is unsuitable for making burrows are used, with Magellanic Penguins nesting on the surface. Breeding success is lower for pairs that breed on the surface, due to higher predation from skuas and gulls, but these nests are still more successful than those in burrows in the Falklands.

It is worrying that the Falklands decline of Magellanic Penguins has not levelled out in the way that it has for Gentoo and Rockhopper Penguins. Diet sample studies show that Magellanic Penguins have a greater level of competition for prey with commercial fishing than Gentoo or Rockhoppers, and this may well explain why they continue to decline. The main impact of the Falkland fishing industry is through the reduction of food abundance, rather than by mortality of birds caught in trawling gear, which is rare.

Some colonies along the Atlantic coast of Argentina have also experienced declines, and these declines are due to a combination of commercial fishing and oil pollution from the deliberate discharge of oily ballast water by tanker traffic.

By contrast to the Falkland Islands, the Argentinean fisheries not only affect penguin populations by reducing food abundance, but also through considerable bi-catch of Magellanic Penguins in trawling gear. The reasons for this are unclear, but are probably related to differences in vessel type, trawl speed, net size and catchment areas.

Fishing vessels are not the only man-made hazard faced by Magellanic Penguins in this region. An active offshore oil and gas industry make pollution from oil a constant risk to penguins. Oil is discharged into the sea both through accidental spillage, and through deliberate operational discharge of oily ballast water from tankers.

An estimated 40,000 Magellanic Penguins are killed by oil pollution every year along the coast of Argentina, representing the main cause of adult mortality in this area. The commencement of oil exploration around the Falkland Islands could mean similar mortality amongst all species of Falkland penguins, unless considerably higher standards to those employed in Argentina are demanded. Unfortunately early indications are not good. During a 5 month period of oil exploration around the Falklands in 1998, no less than three oil spills occurred, killing several hundred penguins, cormorants and other seabirds.

Magellanic Penguins from both the Falkland Islands and South America face natural predators at sea, such as Sea Lions, Leopard Seals and Orcas (killer whales). They also face predation of chicks and eggs by avian predators, such as gulls and skuas, but where the penguins nest in burrows, such predation is greatly reduced.

The Dutch explorer Oliver van Noort records visiting Isla Magdalena during the 16th Century, to collect both penguins and eggs for food. Egging of Magellanic Penguins still occurs in the Falkland Islands, but this is now on a very small scale, and has a negligible affect on overall population trends. Magellanic

Penguins are also killed by crab fishermen around the remoter parts of southern Chile, the penguin carcasses being used to bait their crab pots. This probably has little impact on the overall population, but decimates the breeding sites that are affected.

Magellanic Penguins are generally the most accessible penguins for tourism, but they are also the most nervous. Visitors that approach breeding sites which do not normally have many visitors will send the penguins scurrying into their burrows for safety. Magellanic Penguins do readily adapt to regular visitation however, and become much less nervous with time. Nevertheless, careful control of tourism near Magellanic Penguin burrows needs to be enforced, since burrows will readily collapse if walked over.

Simple fences keeping people just 2 or 3 metres away from burrows is all that is needed, and this can benefit both penguins and tourists. Not only are the penguins protected from being crushed in their burrows, but they also rapidly learn that humans will not enter beyond the fence, and will confidently remain sitting outside their burrows for all to see. By contrast, visitors to unfenced sites will generally see little more than distant penguins scurrying away, or faces looking out from within their burrows.

One of the main affects of terrestrial human activity on Magellanic Penguins in the Falklands, has been through the loss of tussac grass by grazing of livestock. Magellanic Penguins prefer to nest amongst tussac grass for protection, but most of this has now been lost from the mainlands of East and West Falkland, as a result of over-grazing. Tussac grass does still remain on many of the offshore islands however, and efforts are now being made to fence off some mainland sites from livestock, in order to allow regeneration. In areas where this has been done, Magellanic Penguins are often quick to recolonise, as can be seen around Gypsy Cove near Port Stanley.

There is a certain degree of symbiosis between Magellanic Penguins and tussac grass. Not only do the penguins benefit from having dense cover for their nests, giving protection against predation and bad weather, but the tussac grass also benefits.

Penguins feeding at sea later deposit their guano around the burrows, providing nutrients that promote lush growth. In addition, abandoned burrows create traps for seeds, where seedlings can get a foothold, and where they are partially sheltered during the initial stages of growth. This is particularly important in enabling tussac grass to colonise new areas, or enabling recolonisation of old areas that had been converted to heathland by overgrazing.

Dr. Mike Bingham

HUMBOLDT PENGUIN *(Spheniscus humboldti)*

The Humboldt Penguin has a fairly limited distribution, being found only along the Pacific coast of South America, in an area of very low rainfall. It ranges from Isla Foca off the coast of Peru, down to Algarrobo in Chile, with one additional isolated colony further to the south on Isla Punihuil. The total world population of Humboldt Penguins currently stands at around 12,000 breeding pairs, with about 8,000 pairs in Chile and the remaining 4,000 pairs in Peru. The population is currently undergoing a serious decline, and the major causes are thought to be overfishing of prey species, entanglement in fishing nets and commercial guano removal.

HUMBOLDT PENGUIN

The Humboldt Penguin is similar in size to the Magellanic Penguin, having an average length of around 70cm., and an average weight of 4kg. The plumage is also similar, except that the two white bands merge to form one thick band across the throat of the Humboldt. The eyes are reddish brown, and the bill is also slightly larger than that of the Magellanic Penguin. The females are slightly smaller than the males, but have similar plumage.

Egg-laying can occur at any time of year between March and December, although two peaks of activity occur around April and September. It is quite common for Humboldt Penguins to rear two successive broods in a single season, when conditions are favourable. This can result in a yearly cycle which comprises of a 2 month moult period, followed by two 5 month breeding cycles. As a consequence, Humboldt Penguins can be seen around their breeding sites throughout the year. As with all *Spheniscids*, Humboldt Penguins strengthen their pair-bonding by allopreening.

Two equally sized eggs are laid with a four day interval, in burrows, rocky crevices or surface scrapes. Incubation takes about 40 days, with both adults changing incubation duties regularly. The major causes of egg loss are from flooding of nests during ocean storms, accidental breakage, nest desertion, and predation by gulls.

Chicks hatch about two days apart, and are fed on a daily basis, with adults leaving the colony in early morning, and returning with food later the same day. The time spent foraging for food increases as the chicks become larger, and require more food, but adults rarely forage more than 35km from the nest site during chick-rearing.

Chicks remain within the nest until they have fully developed mesoptile plumage. Even then, chicks rarely stray far from the nest prior to fledging. The fluffy mesoptile plumage is browny grey above and creamy white beneath, and in conjunction with metabolic changes, it enables the chick to maintain its own body temperature. This allows both adults to leave the burrow to feed, in order to meet the ever increasing demands placed upon them by the growing chicks. When living in burrows, the chicks have no need to form creches in the way that surface breeding birds do. The very arid climate of the region means that Humboldt nests are not generally at risk from being flooded by heavy rain, except under extreme conditions, but burrows close to shore are occasionally flooded by ocean swells.

The chicks fledge at about 10-12 weeks of age, and leave the breeding site for several months to forage at sea. The fledglings have similar markings to the adults, except that they are drabber and lack the black line down the sides of the abdomen. Breeding success rates can be very variable, but are generally in the range of 0.5 to 1 chick fledged per clutch. Adults show high pair fidelity, with most pair-bonds enduring unless one partner dies. They also show high site fidelity, with males showing higher site fidelity than females.

Once the second brood of chicks have fledged, the adults undertake a two week period of foraging at sea, before returning to undergo their annual moult, which lasts around three weeks. After the moult, adults again leave the colonies for about two weeks, to regain weight and condition, prior to returning to begin courtship once more. Humboldt Penguins are capable of breeding at 2 years of age, and can live to over 30 years of age in captivity, although few would achieve this in the wild.

Adults feed close to shore, taking various species of fish (*Engraulis ringens, Sardinops sagax, Odonthestes r.regia, Normanichthys crockeri* and *Scomberesox sp.*) squid *(Todarodes fillippovae)* and crustaceans. Most foraging is done at depths of less than 60m, often amongst weed beds, but they have been known to reach depths of up to 150m. Foraging rarely occurs more than 35km from the colony during the breeding season, but during the austral winter, birds may migrate several hundred kilometres from the breeding site before returning to breed again.

Map showing world distribution of Humboldt Penguins

The coastline along which the Humboldt Penguin is found is particularly susceptible to the influences of El Niño Southern Oscillation (ENSO) events, which occasionally bring seasons of extreme food shortage. During such years, cool nutrient rich waters which normally flow northwards along the coast of Chile and Peru, become displaced by warmer nutrient poor waters flowing from the central Pacific. This loss of nutrients results in a slowing down of primary production by phytoplankton, which in turn affects the entire marine food chain. Being top predators within the marine ecosystem, penguins are amongst the worst affected species, and often face complete abandonment of breeding, and even possible starvation. The Humboldt Penguins are particularly dependent on the availability of fish, which are forced to move further offshore in search of cooler currents.

Such events are often accompanied by severe weather patterns, which can bring heavy rain and flooding to areas that normally receive little or no rain. Under such conditions, Humboldt breeding sites may be completely washed out, as happened along the coast of Peru during the ENSO of 1997/98.

In addition to natural predators, such as gulls, vultures, caracaras, foxes, pinipeds (seals) and cetaceans, Humboldt Penguins also face a number of man-made hazards. Commercial fishing reduces breeding success and survival rates through depletion of food resources. Overfishing of the Peruvian Anchovy (*Engraulis ringens*) led to its population collapse in the 1970s. This fish was a major component of the Humboldt Penguin diet, and penguin populations suffered as a result.

Hundreds of Humboldt Penguins are also caught and drowned in the nets of local fishermen every year. Accidental entanglement in gill-nets, and the deliberate hunting of adults for food and fishing bait, are the main causes of adult mortality in some areas. Eggs are also taken from many breeding colonies, resulting in disturbance and reduced breeding success.

The breeding habitat of the Humboldt Penguin is also damaged by human activity. The guano which builds up around certain breeding colonies due to the arid climate, is scraped off down to the bare rock for use as fertiliser, leaving nothing for the birds to burrow into. Introduced predators, such as wild dogs, also prevent successful breeding on many mainland sites, restricting most breeding populations to offshore islands or specially protected areas.

Because Humboldt Penguins have such a limited geographic distribution, their numbers are naturally low, and this makes them particularly vulnerable to human disturbance. Unless mitigating measures are taken to reduce the impacts currently being exerted on this small population, the species will be extinct within a few decades.

GALAPAGOS PENGUIN *(Spheniscus mendiculus)*

The Galapagos Penguin has the smallest breeding range and population size of any penguin, with less than a thousand breeding pairs. It only occurs in the Galapagos Islands, with 90% of the population being restricted to the western islands of Fernandina and Isabela.

GALAPAGOS PENGUIN

The Galapagos Penguin is the smallest of the South American penguins, with an average length of less than 50cm, and an average weight of less than 2.5kg. It has a black head and upperparts, with a thin white line running from the throat, up around the head to meet the corner of the eye. The underparts are white, but are bordered by a black line which extends down to the blackish legs. The upper bill and tip of the lower bill are black, with the remainder of the lower bill and surrounding skin around to the eye being pinkish yellow. The females are smaller than the males, but have similar plumage.

Unlike other penguins, Galapagos Penguins have no particular breeding season, and may have as many as three clutches in a single year. This is an adaptation that allows them to take advantage of periods of high food abundance, and to cope with a very variable and unreliable food resource.

Galapagos Penguins undergo their moult prior to breeding, and may moult twice in a single year. Moulting birds generally avoid the water, but because the equatorial waters are warm, birds that become underweight are able to go to sea to feed, rather than face starvation.

By moulting prior to breeding, Galapagos Penguins are able to ensure that early failure of their food resources will not result in starvation during the moult. Should food supplies disappear prior to the completion of breeding, then breeding success will suffer, but the adults will have the highest chance of surviving the shortage. It is the survival of the adult population that ultimately ensures the survival of the species.

Sea surface temperatures around the Galapagos Islands can vary between 15 - 28 degrees Celsius. During periods of high surface water temperature, primary production is low as a result of the nutrient poor waters, and food becomes short. Such periods of extreme food shortage are called El Niño Southern Oscillations (ENSO), and during such seasons penguins postpone breeding completely. It is better to delay breeding than to risk adult starvation, which is still the main cause of adult mortality.

El Niño means "The Boy", and was so named after the Holy Child Jesus Christ because it usually peaks around Christmas time. During ENSO events, cool nutrient rich waters flowing northwards up the coast of Chile and Peru become displaced by warm nutrient poor waters from the central Pacific. The drop in primary production resulting from the low nutrient levels, works its way up through the food chain, causing food shortages for many species that depend on the ocean. The affects of ENSO events are not restricted to the ocean, since weather patterns are also disrupted right across South America and the Caribbean, usually associated with heavy rains.

Breeding is stimulated amongst Galapagos Penguins by a drop in sea surface temperatures to below about 24 degrees Celsius, which corresponds to the presence of nutrient rich currents, and in turn an abundance of prey. Nests are made along turbulent rocky shores within about 50m of the water, mostly on the islands of Fernandina and Isabela. Burrows are sometimes dug in suitable volcanic deposits, but often nests are in caves or crevices in old fissured larva. Adults remain around the breeding sites throughout the year.

Two eggs are laid 4 days apart, but adults do not normally relay if the clutch is lost. Incubation of the eggs takes 38 - 40 days, and is shared equally by both parents. Chicks are brooded for the first 30 days, and this is performed by both parents, with daily change-overs. By the end of the 30 days, the chicks have developed a mesoptile plumage that is brown above and white below, which serves more to protect the chicks from the strong sun than to keep them warm. Both adults are then able to forage for food, but chicks do not form into creches.

Chicks fledge at 60 - 65 days of age, and fledging may occur at any time of year. Fledglings have greyish black upperparts and white underparts, but lack the white lines of the adults. Instead they have paler cheeks which indicate where the thin white head line will later develop.

Pair-bonds are long-lasting, and this allows rapid reproduction when conditions become favourable. Pair-bonding is constantly reinforced by allopreening and bill duelling.

The main problem that Galapagos Penguins face in relation to weather, is from the strong sun. Entering the water enables penguins to cool off, but when on land they have a number of behavioural adaptations that help them to keep cool. Birds can lose heat from the exposed areas of skin on their feet, and the underparts of their flippers, aided by increases in blood flow to these areas. Birds are often seen standing with out-stretched flippers, hunched forward to shade their feet from the sun. They also lose heat by evaporation from the throat and airways through panting.

Galapagos Penguins do not leave the archipelago, and generally forage close to shore in the cooler Cromwell Current, returning to the land at night. Their diet comprises almost entirely of small schooling fish, particularly mullet and sardines of 1 - 15 cm in length, although some crustaceans are also taken. Co-operative feeding is often employed, and foraging is restricted to daylight hours. Foraging rarely occurs more than a few kilometres from the breeding site.

During periods of food shortage, penguins tend to forage individually, and make no attempt to breed until surface waters drop in temperature once more. During 1982/83, an ENSO event hit the Galapagos Islands so badly that around 77% of the penguin population starved to death, and the population has only gradually been showing signs of recovery.

During 1970/71, the population of Galapagos Penguins was estimated at 6,000 to 15,000 birds. During October 1997, an archipelago-wide census conducted by the Charles Darwin Research Station recorded a total population of just 883 adults, with 184 juveniles and 217 birds of undetermined age. Nevertheless, this was 27% greater than a similar census conducted during 1996.

Unlike larger penguins which have few natural predators on land, Galapagos Penguins must guard against crabs, snakes, owls and hawks, although predation from such sources is generally low. At sea Galapagos Penguins may be killed by sharks, fur seals and sea lions. On Isabela, introduced cats, dogs and rats are also predators. In addition to predation, and other natural hazards associated with an unreliable food resource and volcanic activity, they face a number of man-made hazards.

Tourists and illegal sea cucumber fisherman create disturbance, and affect the marine ecosystem. The illegal fisherman chop down and burn mangrove trees in order to cook the sea cucumbers, affecting the penguins' nesting habitat, and both fisherman and tourists discard refuse that regularly entangles and kills unsuspecting birds. Penguins are accidentally caught in fishing nets, and in 2001 an oil spill hit the islands when a tanker ran aground.

The Galapagos Islands are only small, and careful management will be required to balance the increasing pressures from human activities, with the needs of sustaining the fragile and unique ecosystem. With such a small remaining population, the Galapagos Penguin faces the possibility of extinction, unless such a balance can be successfully achieved.

Dr. Mike Bingham

PART 3: Penguins and the Environment

Dr. Mike Bingham

Far from being comical birds, ill-adapted to the rigours of a hostile environment, penguins are in fact the most successful avian predators of the southern oceans, and have remained so for at least 50 million years. Their overall design has changed little during that period, and each of the penguin species are similar in appearance. Nevertheless, each species has adopted individual characteristics which hone their life cycle to the individual nature of their selected niche.

The southern oceans are immensely rich in plankton, and these form the platform upon which all southern ocean foodwebs are built. Penguins sit upon the pinnacle of this food-web, alongside other seabirds, cetaceans and pinipeds (seals). Whilst it is true that certain species of cetaceans and pinipeds will take penguins for food, this forms only of tiny proportion of their normal dietary composition, feeding mainly on squid, fish and crustaceans.

Healthy adult penguins have few natural predators on land, but penguin breeding colonies do help support populations of avian predators and scavengers. Such species generally utilise other food resources during their non-breeding season, when their daily food demands are low, but the increased demands of breeding and chick rearing can be met by rich pickings from penguin colonies.

Penguin chicks are messy feeders, and often drop food scraps during food transfer from the adult. Food dropped onto the ground is not retrieved by the penguins, but is eagerly snatched by waiting gulls, such as Dolphin Gulls (*Larus scoresbii*) and Kelp Gulls (*Larus dominicanus*). In addition, the digestive tract of penguins is not very efficient, and some items of food, such as crustaceans with a hard ectoskeleton, may pass through virtually undigested. Gulls and Snowy Sheathbills (*Chionis alba*) are able to scavenge such scraps, and receive sustenance from them.

In addition to food scraps, penguin eggs and young chicks also offer easy targets to avian predators. Birds such as skuas and caracaras continually watch over penguin colonies in search of unguarded eggs and chicks. Penguin colonies are constantly active, and during the course of territorial squabbles, eggs and chicks are inevitably left unguarded momentarily. Such a brief lapse in concentration is all that a waiting predator needs, and swooping down onto the unattended nest, it will remove the egg or small chick with its bill, and take it to a nearby perch to be dissected.

This time of plenty is essential in providing for the young of such predators, which schedule their own chick-rearing to correspond with this abundance of prey. Nevertheless, such predators are generally opportunistic feeders, being equally at home taking smaller prey, such as invertebrates, or scavenging on dead bird or mammal carcasses. This adaptability is essential around the Falkland Islands and southern South America, where penguin colonies are mostly deserted during the remainder of the year, and other sources of food are needed to sustain such predators. During these winter months there is very little live prey for such species, and carcasses or invertebrates become the primary sources of food.

Penguins link the highly productive marine ecosystems of the southern oceans with the comparatively impoverished terrestrial ecosystems of the subantarctic islands. Feeding entirely at sea, they remove large quantities of energy and nutrients in the form of fish, squid and crustaceans, and allow a large proportion of this to be passed on to terrestrial scavengers, predators, parasites and detritivores.

It is not only the terrestrial fauna that benefits from the presence of penguins. The ground around a penguin colony receives a large input of nutrients as a result of the penguin guano and food scraps that are deposited, and this in turn alters the floral composition.

At the point of deposition such a high concentration of nutrients may kill off some vegetation, but the overall result of this input to the ecosystem is a considerable increase in plant growth. Not only does such an input of nutrients increase overall growth, but it also favours species which are better adapted at converting higher concentrations of nutrients into faster growth. Such species are often excluded under conditions of low nutrient input, since the very qualities that allow them to compete under high nutrient levels, make them poor competitors under low nutrient levels.

The numerous islands of the Falklands and the southern tip of South America have no woodland cover, and are generally dominated by heathland comprising of dwarf shrubs and grasses. Plants adapted to low nutrient levels survive under such conditions by having low rates of growth and metabolism. Such plants are generally of comparatively low nutrient value, often with a high proportion of dead material, making the vegetation look brown or pale in colour. A greater proportion of actively growing cells would require a greater metabolic rate, which cannot be supported by the impoverished soils.

By comparison, the vegetation found around penguin colonies is generally greener, due to the higher proportion of actively growing cells, indicative of species adapted to more rapid growth. Such vegetation is not only comparatively species-rich, but is also more nutritious to grazing birds and animals.

These nutrient rich patches are often called greens, as a result of their brighter colour, and can become mini-ecosystems in their own right. Grazers such as geese and rabbits utilise such areas, and by grazing the vegetation and recycling the nutrients through their droppings, such animals are able to maintain the greens long after the penguins have left. Such areas also support a higher density and diversity of invertebrates, the majority of which are detritivores. These in turn provide rich feeding for smaller birds. Penguin colonies are not the only sources of such greens, but in many areas they are the most common.

Close to the coastal fringe itself, specialist species that are adapted to the salt laden air tend to dominate. The most widespread of these is tussac grass (*Parodiochloa flabellata*). This species is generally able to grow well away from the coast, but is prevented from doing so by more competitive species. Within about 300 metres of the sea however, tussac grass is adapted to out-compete the more generalist species, and becomes dominant, producing a dense thicket of up to 3 metres in height. Such areas may be comparatively poor in terms of floral diversity, but they hold an abundance of invertebrates, most of which are detritivores. In terms of invertebrate biomass, tussac grass is the most productive terrestrial habitat type of the region, and doubtless holds numerous species unknown to science.

Tussac grass provides important habitat for bird species too, some of which feed on the abundance of invertebrates, and others which use the dense cover as protection for nests. Seabirds in particular use offshore tussac islands as breeding grounds.

Penguins do not rely on tussac grass as such, but Magellanic Penguins do have a preference for such habitat when it is available. The deep tussac peat and dense canopy of leaves enables Magellanic Penguins to nest in large numbers at sites that would not otherwise provide suitable habitat for nesting. Many offshore tussac islands around the Falkland Islands and southern Chile would be too rocky, with soils too thin to permit burrowing, were it not for the presence of tussac grass.

The main contribution made to the tussac island ecosystem by penguins, is through the input of nutrients deposited in and around the burrows. Magellanic Penguins are too large and strong to be killed by avian predators, and even their eggs and young are rarely taken from burrows that are so well protected by the dense vegetation. Sea Lions often utilise tussac islands for pupping and as places to haul out, and sometimes they will lie in wait for Magellanic Penguins as they come and go from their breeding sites.

The tussac island ecosystem supports a few grazing invertebrates, but most tussac islands have no other grazing animals. Tussac grass did not developed in the presence of large grazing animals, and it has low tolerance to being grazed. This has become very apparent where man has allowed uncontrolled grazing of tussac grass by livestock. Most of the belts of tussac grass that once surrounded East and West Falkland have now disappeared as a result of livestock grazing, and such areas are now covered by heath and grass, or have become eroded and rocky.

Northwards along the coasts of South America, the climate becomes warmer, and tussac grass gives way to other coastal vegetation types. Along the Atlantic coast of Patagonia, the climate is comparatively dry, and the vegetation is fairly open. Magellanic Penguins continue to make burrows where the soils are sufficiently deep to do so, but otherwise they will nest above ground in shallow depressions or under bushes. As with tussac islands, guano is deposited around the base of such covering vegetation, raising the level of the nutrients in the soil, but the covering vegetation offers much less protection for the nests, and predation is higher.

By comparison to the drier Atlantic coast of Patagonia, the Pacific coast of southern South America receives high annual rainfall. This gives rise to dense scrub and woodland along the labyrinth of uninhabited islands which border the coastline of southern and central Chile. This region holds numerous seabirds, including Sooty Shearwaters (*Puffinus griseus*), White-chinned Petrels (*Procellaria aequinoctialis*) and Magellanic Penguins, which nest under cover of the dense vegetation. The hundreds of islands and channels which make up this vast area are immensely rich in wildlife, and yet are largely unexplored and uncharted.

Further northwards, along the coast of northern Chile and Peru, the climate becomes very dry, and the guano deposited by seabirds is no longer washed away due to the lack of rain. The guano can accumulate into deposits several metres thick, and at some sites the Humboldt Penguins rely on these deposits to provide a substrate into which they can dig their burrows. The value of such deposits for fertiliser has long been recognised, and in many areas they are excavated by man for use in agriculture. Such deposits have often been scraped away down to the underlying bedrock, leaving the penguins without suitable breeding habitat.

Whilst penguins are well adapted to the natural environment in which they live, they are less able to cope with man-made changes to their environment. Agricultural activities have modified the landscape in a number of ways, and these changes have brought about changes for the penguins that rely on such habitat for nesting. The loss of nesting habitat, be it through the excavation of guano or the overgrazing of tussac grass, inevitably restricts the breeding population that a region can support. In general however, penguins are fairly tolerant of human disturbance, and are quite able to live in association with man, provided that their feeding and nesting requirements are not compromised.

Ever since these regions were first occupied, penguin eggs have provided a source of food for human settlements, and the practice still continues to a lesser extent in the Falkland Islands. In general it is the Gentoo egg that is preferred, and given the Gentoo's remarkable ability to relay, the practice has little impact on the total population, provided that it is not carried out on a commercial scale.

Both penguins and seals have thick layers of subcuticular fat which insulate their bodies from the cold waters of the southern ocean. Prior to the availability of petroleum products, this body fat was a highly prized commodity, and huge numbers of seals and penguins were killed and boiled down to extract this oil. Boats from Britain and Europe visited sites such as the Falklands Islands during the last century, and decimated colonies of penguins and seals. The bodies were thrown into huge metal cauldrons called tripots, and heated up until the body fat melted into an oil that was drained off and stored. Even the fires that heated the tripots were fuelled by the bodies of penguins, which were simply thrown onto the open fires.

The fact that penguin populations were healthy at the beginning of the 20th century, despite such heavy exploitation, bears testimony to the immense productivity of the southern oceans. Penguin populations are generally held in check by the availability of food and nesting sites. Although the loss of nesting habitat has undoubtedly had an effect in certain regions, it is generally food availability that controls the overall population size of most penguins. Provided that food availability remains high, then penguins are generally able to tolerate increased levels of mortality and exploitation, but reductions in food availability can have far reaching consequences.

Food availability is a delicate balance, and relates not only to total food availability, but also how such food resources are distributed, and how easily they can be found. Healthy adult penguins generally have little difficulty finding sufficient food to meet their daily needs, but there are occasions when food demands increase dramatically, such as during breeding and prior to moulting.

During the breeding season, one adult must incubate the eggs and young chicks, whilst the partner feeds at sea. Whether change-overs are made on a daily basis, or over a longer time-scale, each penguin must nevertheless find two days worth of food for each day spent foraging. Once the chicks hatch, this demand increases still further, since the chicks must rely on food which is surplus to the adults' requirements. Rapidly growing chicks need large quantities of food to maintain their rapidly growing bodies, and unless this food supply is maintained, they will die. Each adult now needs to catch several times its normal daily requirement in order to successfully raise its brood, and yet in most cases, the range over which it can now forage is restricted to a radius of 30 or 40 km from the nest site.

At large breeding sites, such as Rockhopper colonies, there is considerable competition for food within the feeding grounds close to each colony. Such areas must remain highly productive if the demands of so many penguins are to be met. In general, food is rarely in sufficient abundance to meet the needs of all, and many chicks receive insufficient food and die.

In nests with two chicks, the strongest chick will grab most of the food and grow stronger, whilst the smaller chick grows weaker and dies. Inexperienced adults and adults that are getting old or sick, may have difficulty in catching sufficient food to sustain even one healthy chick. During periods of food shortage, adults can often be seen leaving tiny chicks alone in the nest so that both adults can search for food. This places the chicks in grave danger, but is necessary in order to keep them fed.

During the normal course of events, the balance of chicks that survive are sufficient to replace the adults that die each year, and the population remains in a steady state. If the population is reduced, due to human exploitation or some natural disaster, then the competition for food will be reduced, allowing more chicks to survive, and hence the population to increase until it is once again in balance. This control mechanism is further enhanced through the number of juveniles that survive to breed. It is a time when youngsters must rapidly learn how to feed themselves, whilst competing against experienced adults for food.

If the overall abundance of food is reduced by even a small amount, this balance of chick and juvenile survival will be tilted, and the population will decline. Adult mortality increases slightly, as the very weakest or oldest adults are unable to find sufficient food, perhaps to fatten up for their annual moult. Juvenile mortality increases significantly, as they face greater competition for existing resources from the experienced adult population. Chick production is also reduced considerably, as adults either postpone breeding, or find it more difficult to find the extra food needed to maintain their chicks.

It is perhaps through man's ability to alter the marine food chain that he has had his greatest affect on penguin populations. The Humboldt Penguin population was badly affected by the over-fishing of sardines off the coasts of Chile and Peru, and more recently penguin populations appear to have been affected by commercial fishing for squid and fish around the Falkland Islands.

Since the early 1960s, the waters around the Falkland Islands have attracted fishing boats from around the world. Throughout the 1970s and early 1980s this fishing took place without any regulatory body in place, and the quantities of fish and squid that were taken increased enormously. Throughout this period penguin populations declined, and in the autumn of 1985, huge numbers of adult penguins died from starvation during their annual moult.

The penguins had been unable to find sufficient food to build up their body fat reserves prior to their annual moult, and had starved to death in their thousands at colonies throughout the Falklands. Rockhopper Penguins were the worst affected, losing around 50% of their entire adult population as a result of the event. Following this catastrophe, the Falkland Islands Government established a fisheries conservation zone around the Falkland Islands, and began licensing fishing activities. This not only generated an income to the islands through the sale of licenses, but also allowed the level of fishing activity to be controlled.

No further mass mortalities of penguins occurred, however penguin populations continued to decline throughout the 1980s and early 1990s, largely as a result of low breeding success and juvenile survival. By the late 1990s however, fishing effort had been reduced, and Falkland penguins began to show increases in breeding success. For Gentoo and Rockhopper Penguins these increases in breeding success have been followed by some population recovery.

Gentoo Penguins are able to recover quite quickly from a population decline, as a result of their breeding strategies. During seasons of high food availability, breeding success can exceed 1.5 chicks per nest, and fledglings can return to begin breeding at just two years of age. This has allowed the Falklands' Gentoo population to make a rapid recovery over recent years.

During the austral summer of 1932/33, the Government Naturalist of the Falkland Islands, Mr. A. G. Bennett, undertook a census of Falkland Island penguins, and estimated a Gentoo population of around 116,000 breeding pairs. In 1984 a population study by Dr John Croxall of the British Antarctic Survey reported a similar figure, but by the time of the 1995 population census conducted by the author, the population had declined to 65,000 pairs.

Continued monitoring of selected sites around the Falkland Islands show that the population had levelled out by the end of the 1990s, albeit at a lower level than prior to commercial fishing. Analysis of breeding success over this period shows that the population recovery in the late 1990s closely followed an increase in breeding success. Breeding success is called productivity, and is measured as the average number of chicks that survive to fledge per breeding pair.

The Gentoo population still remains well below the 116,000 breeding pairs recorded by Bennett, but whilst commercial fishing continues to remove food upon which the population relies, it is unlikely to return to such a level. The population should instead reach a new level that is in balance with the food availability existing under the current fisheries regime, all other factors being equal (which they seldom are in ecology - changes in one area of the food chain often have unexpected consequences elsewhere).

By comparison to the opportunistic breeding strategy of the Gentoo, Rockhopper Penguins concentrate on rearing one healthy chick under a wide range of conditions, and therefore display only slight increases in breeding success during years of high food abundance.

The very large Rockhopper breeding colonies create greater competition for food resources amongst members of the same colony. This may well make them more vulnerable to reductions in food availability, and might explain why the Falklands decline of Rockhoppers was so much more severe than that observed for Gentoos. Unlike Gentoos, Rockhopper Penguins are unable to change the location of their breeding site in response to changes in food availability.

The 1932/33 census conducted by Bennett, recorded a Rockhopper population well in excess of 3 million breeding pairs. In 1984 Croxall recorded a population of 2.5 million breeding pairs, but by the time of the 1995 census conducted by the author, the population had crashed to just 297,000 pairs, a decline of 88% in 11 years.

Continued monitoring since 1995 has shown a slight recovery to around 350,000 pairs by the end of the 1990s. Populations now appear to be stable, but it is extremely unlikely that populations will ever return to their former level whilst commercial fishing continues. The population appears to have declined to the point where it is in balance with the level of food available under the current fishing regime. With careful management of commercial fishing, the remaining population of Rockhopper Penguins could perhaps exist in harmony. Unfortunately this may not be the case for Magellanic Penguins.

Diet sample studies show that Magellanic Penguins have greater reliance on Loligo squid and Blue Whiting (fish), two of the main target species of the Falklands commercial fishing industry. Magellanic Penguins declined by 70% in the Falklands during the 1990s alone. Allowing for declines during the 1980s, the total decline probably exceeds 90%. Despite this huge decline, populations have not reached equilibrium, and are still falling.

Comparison with populations on Isla Magdalena (Chile) where commercial fishing is not permitted, supports the hypothesis that a reduction of prey is leading to poor breeding success in the Falklands. On Isla Magdalena, adults are able to find sufficient food for their chicks in about 18 hours, but around the Falklands they require an average of 35 hours. Chicks are therefore receiving half as much food in the Falklands, and research shows that chick survival is greatly reduced as a result. Magellanic Penguins rear an average of 0.82 chicks per nest in the Falklands, compared to 1.35 chicks on Isla Magdalena This huge reduction in breeding success is sufficient to account for the gradual decline in population, with insufficient chicks being reared in the Falklands to replace natural adult mortality.

The timing of Bennett's Falkland Islands census was particularly fortuitous, since it post-dates the end of the killing of penguins for oil, and pre-dates the establishment of a commercial fishing industry. During the 1930s, direct exploitation of penguins was limited to the taking of eggs for human consumption. Even this was generally restricted to those colonies close to settlements, and the overall impact of such a practice on the population as a whole would have been minimal, especially when one considers the huge quantity of eggs taken by natural predators.

Despite the slaughter of so many penguins for oil during the 19th Century, penguin populations still seemed very healthy during Bennett's census of 1932/33. The Rockhopper Penguin in particular was incredibly numerous, but following the establishment of a fishing industry, this population was reduced to just 10% of its former size.

Other than through the depletion of food resources by commercial fishing, man has not greatly impacted on Falklands penguin populations during that period. The few natural predators of adult penguins have also declined, and in the case of the Southern Sea Lion, the population now stands at just 1% of its former level. Elephant Seals have also declined by around 90% over the last 10 years. Sealions and Elephant Seals both feed primarily on fish and squid.

Out of a total of seven main species of penguin and seal in the Falklands, five compete with the commercial fishing industry for food, and two do not. The five species that do compete have all undergone major population declines since the establishment of the Falklands fishing industry. None of these species have shown these declines in their breeding ranges outside of the Falklands. The problem has been unique to the Falklands, not part of any global trend. The two Falklands species which do not compete for food with commercial fishing (King Penguin and Fur Seal) have both increased in number over recent years.

The last few years have seen a big increase in the number of wildlife tourists, not just in the Falklands and Galapagos Islands, but throughout South America, and naturally penguins feature highly on the agenda. In actual fact, penguins are highly adaptable to human presence, and this makes them ideally suited to tourism. Provided that tourists remain just a few metres outside the periphery of the nesting area, penguins will readily go about their business without concern. This is especially so for colonies that regularly have visitors, since the penguins readily become accustomed to human presence. Very often penguins will approach tourists in order to get a better look at these strange beings.

The author has carried out numerous studies to investigate differences in breeding success between colonies which receive large numbers of tourists, and those which have no tourism. Perhaps surprisingly, there is no apparent decrease in breeding success for colonies with tourists, provided that people do not enter the nesting area, and a number of sites show slightly higher breeding success as a result of tourism.

This may be because the natural predators of penguin eggs and chicks, such as skuas, caracaras, and even foxes in South America, are kept at bay by human presence. This is all to the benefit of the penguins, although the populations of predators could suffer if tourism were widespread. In general, however, only a very small percentage of breeding sites are actually visited.

Penguins have always been a huge attraction at zoos, and it is good that visitors are also able to see these fascinating creatures in their natural setting. Only by seeing penguins in the flesh can one really appreciate their charm.

A penguin colony is an amazing place. It is never still; always full of hustle and bustle, adults coming and going, calling, squabbling, and dashing about on errands that to our eyes seem completely random. The chicks look so comical too, having bodies that seem out of proportion with their legs. During the early stages of development they are little more than stomachs on legs, with open beaks demanding ever more food to be stuffed inside.

For all their comical mannerisms, penguins are perfectly adapted to the environment in which they live; a half-life between land and water. Of all the animals that live on both land and in the ocean, penguins are perhaps the most successful at adapting to both. They can out-swim most fish, and out-run many a man. They can survive in the coldest climates on earth, and on the equator.

But for all their hardiness, penguins are still very vulnerable. Their success ultimately depends on being able to find sufficiently high concentrations of fish and squid to survive and to raise young. Whilst food resources are retained, penguin populations are able to survive moderate levels of exploitation and disturbance. However when food resources are depleted, by natural phenomena such as ENSO events, or by over exploitation of fish and squid stocks, the inevitable result is the decline of the penguin.

For species that are widespread and numerous, events that impact on the population in one area may not threaten the overall population if other areas remain unaffected. The Southern Rockhopper and Magellanic Penguins, whose populations have crashed in the Falkland Islands, have remained largely unaffected throughout their breeding range in South America.

Species which have a limited distribution, however, are very vulnerable to changes to their ecosystem. The Galapagos Penguin was hit hard during the ENSO event of 1982/83, and whilst struggling to recover, it was hit by oil pollution from a tanker than ran aground in 2001. Similarly the Humboldt Penguin has declined sharply as a result of over-fishing of Peruvian Anchovy stocks during the 1970s, and its population is further threatened by a multitude of man-made changes to its breeding environment.

Given half a chance, penguins are very able to adapt to human disturbance, but we need to be aware of their needs, and of how easily we can disrupt fragile ecosystems. Continued monitoring and research is essential in gauging the health of penguin populations, and for identifying conflicts with human needs at an early stage, so that the consequential damage of our activities can be minimised.

Nevertheless, penguins are far more than a subject for study; they are a valued part of our natural world. They hold a place in the hearts of children, and act as monitors of the health of our southern oceans. They are an important link in the ecosystem of our planet, and so are we. The world is left poorer for the passing of a single species, and yet this power lies in the hands of each and every one of us.

Whilst human populations increase, and our thirst for natural resources continues, then conservation may amount to no more than rearranging the furniture on the *Titanic*. It is all too easy to think that our own individual life styles contribute little, or that we will change when others do, but each grain of sand makes up the beach.

Dr. Mike Bingham

PART 4: Bibliography

Dr. Mike Bingham

Adams, N.J. - (1987) Foraging ranges of King Penguins during summer at Marion Island. *Journal of Zoology, London*, 212: 475-482.

Adams, N.J. - (1992) Embryonic metabolism, energy budgets and cost of production of King and Gentoo Penguin eggs. *Comparative Biochemistry and Physiology*, 101A: 497-503.

Adams, N.J. and Brown, C.R. - (1983) Diving depths of the Gentoo Penguin, *Condor*, 85: 503-504.

Adams, N.J. and Brown, C.R. - (1990) Energetics of moult in penguins. In *Penguin biology* (ed. L.S. Davis and J.T. Darby), 297-315. Academic Press, San Diego.

Adams, N.J. and Klages, N.T. - (1987) Seasonal variation in the diet of the King Penguin at sub-Antarctic Marion Island. *Zoological Society of London*, 212: 303-324.

Adams, N.J. and Klages, N.T. - (1989) Temporal variation in the diet of the Gentoo Penguin at Marion Island. *Colonial Waterbirds*, 12: 30-36

Adams, N.J. and Wilson, M.P. - (1987) Foraging parameters of Gentoo Penguins at sub-Antarctic Marion Island. *Polar Biology*, 7: 51-56.

Araya, B. and Todd, F.S. - (1988) Status of the Humboldt Penguin in Chile following the 1982-83 El Niño. *Spheniscid Penguin Newsletter*, 1(1): 8-10.

Aubert de la Rüe, E. - (1959) Quelque observations faites aux iles Diego Ramirez (Chile). *Bulletin of the Natural History Museum.* 31(4): 387-391. Paris.

Badano, L.A., Scolaro, J.A. and Upton, J.A. - (1982) Distribución especial de la nidificacion de *Spheniscus magellanicus* en Cabo Dos Bahias, Chubut, Argentina. *Historia Natural*, 2: 241-251.

Baldwin, J., Jardel, J.P., Montague, T. and Tomkin, R. - (1984) Energy metabolism in penguin swimming muscles. *Molecular Physiology*, 6: 33-42.

Barré, H. - (1984) Metabolic and insulative changes in winter and summer acclimatised King Penguin chicks. *Journal of Comparative Physiology B,* 154: 317-324.

Barré, H. and Roussel, B. - (1986) Thermal and metabolic adaptation to first cold-water immersion in juvenile penguins. *American Journal of Physiology,* 251: R456-462.

Bennett, A.G. - (1933) *The penguin population of the Falkland Islands in 1932/33.* Government Report, Falkland Islands.

Bennett, K. - (1993) Behavioural observations of captive Magellanic Penguins with chicks. *Penguin Conservation,* 6: 7-12.

Bingham, M. - (1994) Falklands Conservation population report. *Penguin News,* Vol.6, No.4: 9.

Bingham, M. - (1994) Conservation Report on Magellanic Penguins. *Penguin News,* Vol.6, No.20: 10.

Bingham, M. - (1994) Conservation Report on Rockhopper Penguins. *Penguin News,* Vol.6, No.21: 9.

Bingham, M. - (1994) Gentoo Penguin population trends: 1987/88 - 1993/94, *The Warrah,* 5: 4-5.

Bingham, M. - (1994) Penguin Report: food for thought. *The Warrah,* 6: 8-10.

Bingham, M. - (1995) Population status of penguin species in the Falkland Islands. *Penguin Conservation,* 8(1): 14-19.

Bingham, M. - (1995) Seabird Surveys. *The Warrah,* 7: 5.

Bingham, M. - (1996) Penguin population census 1995-96. *The Warrah,* 10: 6-7.

Bingham, M. - (1997) Observations of food transfer between Gentoo Penguin siblings. *Marine Ornithology,* 25(1).

Bingham, M. - (1998) Penguins of South America and the Falkland Islands. *Penguin Conservation,* 11(1): 8-15.

Bingham, M. - (1998) The distribution, abundance and population trends of Gentoo, Rockhopper and King Penguins in the Falkland Islands. *Oryx,* 32(3): 223-32.

Bingham, M. - (2000) Field Guide to Birds of the Falkland Islands. ERU Publications Ltd., Stanley, Falkland Islands

Bingham, M. and Mejias, E. - (1999) Penguins of the Magellan Region. *Scientia Marina,* Vol: 63, Supl. 1

Blanco, D.E., Yorio, P. and Boersma, P.D. - (1996) Feeding behaviour, size asymmetry, and food distribution in Magellanic Penguin chicks. *Auk,* 113: 496-498.

Boersma, P.D. - (1974) The Galapagos Penguin: a study of adaptations for life in an unpredictable environment. Ph.D. thesis. Ohio State University, Columbus.

Boersma, P.D. - (1975) Adaptation of Galapagos Penguins for life in two different environments. In *The Biology of Penguins,* (ed. B. Stonehouse), 101-114. Macmillan, London.

Boersma, P.D. - (1976) An ecological and behavioural study of the Galapagos Penguin. *Living Bird,* 15: 43-93.

Boersma, P.D. - (1978) Breeding patterns of Galapagos Penguins as an indicator of oceanic conditions. *Science,* 200: 1481-1483.

Boersma, P.D. - (1987) Penguins oiled in Argentina. *Science,* 236: 135.

Boersma, P.D. - (1987) El Niño behind penguin deaths? *Nature,* 327: 96.

Boersma, P.D. - (1988) Census of Magellanic Penguins at Punta Tombo, Argentina. *Pacific Seabird Group Bulletin,* 15: 22.

Boersma, P.D. - (1991) Asynchronous hatching and food allocation in the Magellanic Penguin. *Acta Congressus Internationalis Ornithologici,* XX: 961-973.

Boersma, P.D. - (1991) Nesting sites for *Spheniscus* penguins. *Spheniscus Penguin Newsletter,* 4: 8-9.

Boersma, P.D. - (1997) Magellanic Penguins decline in South Atlantic. *Penguin Conservation,* 10(1): 2-5.

Boersma, P.D., Stokes, D.L. and Yorio, P.M. - (1990) Reproductive variability and historical change of Magellanic Penguins at Punta Tombo, Argentina. In *Penguin Biology,* (ed. L.S. Davis and J.T. Darby) 15-43, Academic Press, San Diego.

Boersma, P.D. and Stokes, D.L. - (1996) Mortality patterns, hatching asynchrony, and size asymmetry in Magellanic Penguin chicks. In *The Penguins: Ecology and Management,* (ed. P. Dann, I. Norman and P. Reilley), Surrey Beatty and Sons, NSW.

Boersma, P.D., Yorio, P., Gandini, P. and Frere, E. - (1995) Close encounters in Chubut. *América,* 47: 26-35.

Bost, C.A. and Jouventin, P. - (1990) Evolutionary ecology of the Gentoo Penguin. In *Penguin Biology,* (ed. L.S. Davis and J.T. Darby), 85-112, Academic Press, San Diego.

Bost, C.A. and Jouventin, P. - (1990) Laying asynchrony in Gentoo Penguins on Crozet Island: causes and consequences. *Ornis Scandinavica,* 21: 63-70.

Bost, C.A. and Jouventin, P. - (1991) The breeding performance of the Gentoo Penguin at the northern edge of its range. *Ibis,* 133: 14-25.

Bost, C.A. and Jouventin, P. - (1991) Relationship between fledging weight and food availability in seabirds: is the Gentoo Penguin a good model? *Oikos,* 60: 113-114.

Bost, C.A., Koubbi, P., Genevois, F., Ruchon, L. and Ridoux, V. - (1994) Gentoo Penguin diet as an indicator of planktonic availability in the Kerguelen Islands. *Polar Biology,* 14: 147-153.

Bost, C.A. *et al* - (1997) Foraging habitat and food intake of satellite-tracked King Penguins during the austral summer at Crozet Archipelago. *Marine Ecology Prog. Ser.*

Boswall, J. and Prytherch, R.J. - (1972) Some notes on the birds of Punta Tombo, Argentina. *Bulletin of the British Ornithologists Club*, 92: 118-129.

Boswall, J. and MacIver, D. - (1975) The Magellanic Penguin. In *The biology of Penguins,* (ed. B. Stonehouse), 271-305, Macmillan, London.

Bowmaker, J.K. and Martin, G.R. - (1985) Visual pigments and oil droplets in the penguin, *Spheniscus humboldti. Journal of Comparative Physiology A,* 156: 71-77.

Brown, C.R. - (1984) Resting metabolic rate and energetic cost of incubation in Macaroni and Rockhopper Penguins. *Comparative Biochemistry and Physiology,* 77A: 345-350.

Brown, C.R. - (1985) Energetic cost of moult in Macaroni and Rockhopper Penguins. *Journal of Comparative Physiology B,* 155: 515-520.

Brown, C.R. - (1986) Feather growth, mass loss and duration of moult in Macaroni and Rockhopper Penguins. *Ostrich,* 57: 180-184.

Brown, C.R. - (1987) Travelling speed and foraging range of Macaroni and Rockhopper Penguins at Marion Island. *Journal of Field Ornithology,* 58: 118-125.

Brown, C.R. - (1989) Energy requirements and food consumption of *Eudyptes* penguins at the Prince Edward Islands. *Antarctic Science,* 1: 15-21.

Brown, C.R. and Klages, N. - (1987) Seasonal and annual variation in diets of Macaroni and Southern Rockhopper Penguins at sub-Antarctic Marion Island. *Journal of Zoology,* London, 212: 7-28.

Budd, G.M. - (1975) The King Penguin at Heard Island. In *The biology of penguins,* (ed. B. Stonehouse), 337-352, Macmillan, London.

Burger, A.E. and Williams, A.J. - (1979) Egg temperatures of the Rockhopper Penguin and some other penguins. *Auk,* 96: 100-105.

Campbell, D.G. - (1992) *The Crystal Desert: summers in Antarctica.* Houghton Mifflin, Boston.

Capurro, A., Frere, E., Gandini, M., Gandini, P., Holik, T., Lichtschein, V. and Gregorio, C. - (1986) Radioactividad o hambre. *Propuesta Patagónica,* 4: 16-18.

Capurro, A., Frere, E., Gandini, M., Gandini, P., Holik, T., Lichtschein, V., and Boersma, P.D. - (1988) Nest density and population size of Magellanic Penguins at Cabo Dos Bahias, Argentina. *Auk,* 105: 585-588.

Carribero, A., Perez, D. and Yorio, P.M. - (1995) Actualización del estado poblacional del Pingüino Patagónico *(Spheniscus magellanicus)* en Península Valdés, Chubut, Argentina. *Hornero,* 14(1): 33-38.

Cherel, Y. and Le Maho, Y. - (1985) Five months of fasting in King Penguin chicks: body mass loss and fuel metabolism. *American Journal of Physiology,* 249: R387-392.

Cherel, Y. and Ridoux, V. - (1992) Prey species and nutritive value of food fed during summer to King Penguin chicks at Possession Island, Crozet Archipelago. *Ibis,* 134: 118-127.

Cherel, Y., Stahl, J.C. and Le Maho, Y. - (1987) Ecology and physiology of fasting in King Penguin chicks. *Auk,* 104: 254-262.

Cherel, Y., Robin, J.P., Walche, O., Karmann, H., Netchitailo, P. and Le Maho, Y. - (1988) Fasting in King Penguins I: Hormonal and metabolic changes during breeding. *American Journal of Physiology,* 254: R170-177.

Cherel, Y., Robin, J.P. and Le Maho, Y. - (1988) Physiology and biochemistry of long-term fasting in birds. *Canadian Journal of Zoology,* 66: 159-166.

Cherel, Y., Leloup, J. and Le Maho, Y. - (1988) Fasting in King Penguins II: Hormonal and metabolic changes during moulting. *American Journal of Physiology,* 254: R178-184.

Cherel, Y., Mauget, R., Lacroix, A. and Gilles, J. - (1994) Seasonal and fasting-related changes in circulating gonadal steroids and prolactin in King Penguins. *Physiological Zoology,* 67: 1154-1173.

Clancey, P.A. - (1966) On the penguins *Spheniscus demersus* and *Spheniscus magellanicus* (Forster). *Ostrich,* 37: 237.

Clark, G. - (1988) *The Totorore Voyage.* Century Hutchinson. 357pp.

Clark, G.S., Goodwin, A.J. and Von Meyer, A.P. - (1984) Extension of the known range of some seabirds on the coast of Southern Chile. *Notornis,* 31: 320-334.

Clark, G.S., Cowan, A., Harrison, P. and Bourne W.R.P. - (1992) Notes on the seabirds of the Cape Horn Islands. *Notornis,* 39: 133-144.

Clark, R. - (1986) *Aves de Tierra del Fuego y Cabo de Hornos.* l.o.l.o.

Cocker, R.E. - (1919) Habits and economic relations of the guano birds of Peru. *Proceedings of the United States National Museum,* 56: 449-511.

Conway, W.G. - (1965) The penguin metropolis of Punto Tombo. *Animal Kingdom,* 68: 115-123.

Cooper, J., Brown, C.R., Gales, R.P., Hindell, M.A., Klages, N.T.W., Moors, P.J., Pemberton, D., Ridoux, V., Thompson, K.R. and Van Heezik, Y.M. - (1990) Diets and dietary segregation of crested penguins. In *Penguin Biology,* (ed. L.S. Davis and J.T. Darby), 131-156, Academic Press, San Diego.

Cooper, W. - (1992) Rockhopper Penguins at the Auckland Islands. *Notornis,* 39: 66-67.

Coulter, M.C. - (1984) Seabird conservation in the Galapagos Islands, Ecuador. In *Status and conservation of the world's seabirds,* ICBP Technical Publication No.2, (ed. J.P. Croxall, P.G.H. Evans and R.W. Schreiber), 237-244, ICBP, Cambridge.

Croxall, J.P. - (1982) Energy costs of incubation and moult in petrels and penguins. *Journal of Animal Ecology,* 51: 177-194.

Croxall, J.P. - (1984) Seabirds. In *Antarctic ecology,* Vol.2, (ed. R.M. Laws), 533-619, Academic Press, London.

Croxall, J.P. - (1992) Southern Ocean environmental change: effects on seabird, seal and whale populations. *Philosophical Transactions of the Royal Society of London B,* 338: 319-328.

Croxall, J.P, and Davis, R.W. - (1990) Metabolic rate and foraging behaviour of *Pygoscelis* and *Eudyptes* penguins at sea. In *Penguin biology,* (ed. L.S. Davis and J.T. Darby), 207-228, Academic Press, San Diego.

Croxall, J.P. and Furse, J.R. - (1980) Food of Chinstrap Penguins and Macaroni Penguins at Elephant Island, South Shetland Islands. *Ibis,* 122: 237-245.

Croxall, J.P. and Lishman, G.S. - (1987) The food and feeding of penguins. In *Seabirds: feeding ecology and role in marine ecosystems,* (ed. J.P. Croxall), 101-133, Cambridge University Press.

Croxall, J.P. and Prince, P.A. - (1980) The food of the Gentoo Penguin and Macaroni Penguin at South Georgia. *Ibis,* 122: 245-253.

Croxall, J.P., McInnes, S.J. and Prince P.A. - (1984) The status and conservation of seabirds at the Falkland Islands. In *Status and conservation of the world's seabirds,* ICBP Technical Publication No.2, (ed. J.P. Croxall, P.G.H. Evans and R.W. Schreiber), 271-291, ICBP, Cambridge.

Croxall, J.P., Prince, P.A., Baird A. and Ward P. - (1985) The diet of the Southern Rockhopper Penguin at Beauchene Island, Falkland Islands. *Zoological Society of London,* 206: 485-496.

Croxall, J.P., Davis, R.W. and O'Connell, M.J. - (1988) Diving patterns in relation to diet of Gentoo and Macaroni Penguins at South Georgia. *Condor,* 90: 157-167.

Croxall, J.P., Briggs, D.R., Kato, A., Naito, Y., Watanuki, Y. and Williams T.D. - (1993) Diving pattern and performance in the Macaroni Penguin. *Zoological Society of London,* 230: 31-47.

Croxall, J.P. and Rothery, P. - (1995) Population change in Gentoo Penguins at South Georgia: potential roles of adult survival, recruitment and deferred breeding. In *Penguin biology: Advances in research and management,* (ed. P. Dann, I. Norman and P. Reilly), 26-38. Surrey Beatty, Australia.

Croxall, J.P. (ed.) - 1997. Penguin Conservation Assessment: Antarctic and Subantarctic Species. In: Ellis, S. (ed.) *Penguin Conservation Assessment,* IUCN Conservation Breeding Specialist Group.

Csirke, J. - (1987) Los recursos pesqueros patagónicos y las pesquerías de altura en el Atlántico Sudoccidental. *FAO. Doc. Tec. Pesca,* 286: 1-78.

Culik, B.M. - (1993) Energetics of the *Pygoscelid* penguins. Unpublished thesis. University of Kiel.

Culik, B.M. - (1997) Humboldt penguins at sea: quo vardis? *Penguin Conservation,* 10 (2): 2.

Culik, B.M. and Wilson, R.P. - (1991) Penguins crowded out? *Nature,* 351: 340.

Culik, B.M. and Wilson, R.P. - (1995) Penguins disturbed by tourists. *Nature,* 376: 301-302.

Culik, B.M. and Luna-Jorquera, G. - (1997) Satellite tracking of Humboldt penguins in Northern Chile. *Marine Biology,* 128: 547-556.

Culik, B.M. and Luna-Jorquera, G. - (1997) The Humboldt penguin: a migratory bird? *Journal für Ornithologie,* 138: 325-330

Culik, B.M. and Luna-Jorquera, G. - (In press) Humboldt penguins monitored via VHF-telemetry. *Marine Ecology Program Service.*

Culik, B.M., Wilson, R.P., Dannfeld, R., Adelung, D., Spairani, H.J. and Coria, N.R. - (1991) *Pygoscelid* penguins in a swim canal. *Polar Biology,* 11: 277-282.

Culik, B.M. *et al.* - (1996) Diving energetics in King Penguins. *Journal of Experimental Biology,* 199: 973-983.

Culik, B.M. *et al* - (1996) Core temperature variability in diving King Penguins: a preliminary analysis. *Polar Biology,* 16: 371-378.

Cunningham, D.M. and Moors, P.J. - (1994) The decline of Rockhopper Penguins at Campbell Island, Southern Ocean, and the influence of rising sea temperatures. *Emu,* 94: 27-36.

Cushing, D.H. - (1982) *Climate and fisheries.* Academic Press, London.

Daciuk, J. - (1977) Notas faunísticas y bioecológicas de Península Valdés y Patagonia 6. Observaciónes sobre areas de nidificación de la avifauna del littoral maritimo patagonico. *Hornero,* 11: 361-376.

Davis, R.W., Croxall, J.P. and O'Connell, M.J. - (1989) The reproductive energetics of Gentoo and Macaroni penguins at South Georgia. *Journal of Applied Ecology,* 58: 59-74.

deBary, S.P. - (1990) Influence of nest-site characteristics on the reproductive success of Magellanic penguins. Unpublished MSc. thesis. University of Washington.

de Lisle, G.W., Stanislawek, W.L. and Moors, P.J. - (1990) *Pasteurella multocida* infections in Rockhopper Penguins from Campbell Island, New Zealand. *Journal of Wildlife Disease,* 26: 283-285.

del Hoyo, J., Elliott, A. and Sargatal, J. (ed.) - (1992) *Handbook of birds of the world,* Vol. 1. Lynx Editions, Barcelona.

Derenne, M., Jouventin, P. and Mougin, J.L. - (1979) Le chant du manchot royal (*Aptenodytes patagonicus)* et sa signification évolutive. *Le Gerfaut,* 69: 211-224.

Despin, B. - (1972) Note préliminaire sur le manchot papou *Pygoscelis papua* de l'ile de la Possession (archipel Crozet). *L'Oiseau et la Revue Francaise d'Ornithologie,* 42: 69-83.

Duchamp, C., Barre, H., Delage, D., Bernes, G., Brebion, P. and Rouanet, J. - (1988) Non-shivering thermogenesis in winter-acclimatized King Penguin chicks. In *Physiology of cold adaptation in birds,* (ed. C. Bech and R.E. Reinertsen), 59-67. Plenum Press, New York.

Duffy, D.C. - (1983) Competition for nesting space among Peruvian guano birds. *Auk,* 100: 680-688.

Duffy, D.C. - (1983) The foraging ecology of Peruvian seabirds. *Auk,* 100: 800-810.

Duffy, D.C. and Siegfried, W.R. - (1987) Historical variation in food consumption by breeding seabirds of the Humboldt and Benguela upwelling regions. In *Seabirds: feeding ecology and role in marine ecosystems,* (ed. J.P. Croxall), 327-346. Cambridge University Press.

Duffy, D.C., Hays, C. and Plenge, M.A. - (1984) The conservation status of Peruvian seabirds. In *Status and conservation of the world's seabirds,* ICBP Technical Publication No.2, (ed. J.P. Croxall, P.G.H. Evans and R.W. Schreiber), 245-259, ICBP, Cambridge.

Duffy, D.C., Arntz, W.E., Boersma, P.D. and Morton, R.L. - (1987) The effect of El Niño and the Southern Oscillation on seabirds in the Atlantic Ocean compared to events in Peru. *Proceedings of the 1986 International Ornithological Congress,* Christchurch, New Zealand.

Fordyce, R.C., Jones, C.M. and Field, B.D. - (1986) The world's oldest penguin? *Geological Society of New Zealand Newsletter,* 74: 56.

Fowler, G.S. - (1993) *Ecological and endocrinological aspects of long-term pair bonds in the Magellanic Penguin.* Ph.D thesis. University of Washington, Seattle.

Fowler, G.S. - (1993) Field studies, tourism and stress responses in Magellanic Penguins. In *Report: Workshop on researcher-seabird interactions, 44.* (eds. W.R. Fraser and W.Z. Trivelpiece), Minesota, USA.

Fowler, G.S., Wingfield, J.C., Boersma, P.D. and Sosa, A.R. - (1994) Reproductive endocrinology and weight change in relation to reproductive success in the Magellanic Penguin. *General and Comparative Endocrinology,* In Press.

Fraser, W.R., Trivelpiece, W.Z., Ainley, D.G. and Trivelpiece, S.G. - (1992) Increases in Antarctic penguin populations: reduced competition with whales or a loss of sea ice due to environmental warming? *Polar Biology,* 11: 525-531.

Frere, E. - (1993) Ecologia reproductiva del pingüino de magellanes *(Spheniscus magellanicus)* en la colonia de cabo virgenes. Unpublished thesis. University of Buenos Aires.

Frere, E. and Gandini, P.A. - (1991) La expansión de la gaviota común y su influencia sobre la nidificación del Pingüino de Magellanes. *IV Congreso de Ornitología Neotropical.*

Frere, E., Gandini, P. and Boersma, P.D. - (1992) Effects of nest type and location on reproductive success of the Magellanic Penguin. *Marine Ornithology,* 20: 1-6.

Frere, E., Gandini, M., Gandini, P., Holik, T., Lichtschein V. and Day M.O. - (1993) Variación anual en el número de adultos reproductivos en una nueva colonia de pingüino penacho amarillo en Isla Pingüino (Santa Cruz, Argentina). *Hornero,* 13: 293

Frere, E., Gandini P., and Lichtschein V. - (1997) Variación latitudinal en la dieta del Pingüino de Magallanes en la costa Patagonica, Argentina. *Ornithologia Neotropical.*

Gales, R. and Pemberton, D. - (1988) Recovery of the King Penguin population on Heard Island. *Australian Wildlife Research,* 15: 575-585.

Gales, R., Green, B., Libke, J., Newgrain, K. and Pemberton, D. - (1993) Breeding energetics and food requirements of Gentoo Penguins at Heard and Macquarie Islands. *Journal of Zoology,* London. 231: 125-139.

Gandini, P. - (1993) Patrones de nidificación en el pingüino de magellanes *(Spheniscus magellanicus)* : Efectos de la calidad de habitat y calidad de nido sobre su éxito reproductivo. Unpublished thesis. Universidad de Buenos Aires.

Gandini, P., Boersma, P.D., Frere, E., Gandini, M., Holik, T. and Lichtschein, V. - (1994) Magellanic Penguins are affected by chronic petroleum pollution along the coast of Chubut, Argentina. *Auk,* 111(1): 20-27.

Gandini, P., Frere E. and Boersma P.D. - (1997) Status and conservation of Magellanic Penguins in Patagonia, Argentina. *Bird Conservation International.*

Ghebremeskel, K. *et al.* - (1989) Liver and plasma retinol (vitamin A) in wild, and liver retinol in captive penguins. *Journal of Zoology,* London. 219: 245-250.

Dr. Mike Bingham

Ghebremeskel, K. *et al.* - (1989) Plasma chemistry of Rockhopper, Magellanic and Gentoo wild penguins in relation to moult. *Comparative Biochemistry and Physiology,* 92A 1: 43-47.

Gochfeld, M. - (1980) Timing of breeding and chick mortality in central and peripheral nests of Magellanic Penguins. *Auk,* 97: 191-193.

Gosztonyi, A.E. - (1984) La alimentación del pingüino magellanico *(Spheniscus magellanicus)* en las adyacencias de Punta Tombo, Chubut, Argentina. *Ciencias Nacionales. Patagonia Contribuciones,* 95: 1-19.

Green, B. and Gales, R.P. - (1990) Water, sodium and energy turnover in free-living penguins. In *Penguin biology,* (ed. L.S. Davis and J.T. Darby), 245-268, Academic Press, San Diego.

Guinet, C. *et al* - (1997) Foraging behaviour of satellite-tracked King Penguins in relation to the sea surface temperature obtained by satellite telemetry at Crozet Archipelago during the austral summer: a three year study. *Marine Ecology Prog. Ser.*

Gwynn, A.M. - (1953) The egg-laying and incubation periods of Rockhopper, Macaroni and Gentoo Penguins. A.N.A.R.E. Report (Zool).(B), 1: 1-29.

Gwynn, A.M. - (1993) Clutch size in *Eudyptes* penguins. *Emu,* 93: 287-290.

Gwynn, A.M. - (1993) Egg composition in the Macaroni Penguin. *Emu,* 93: 290-292.

Haftorn, S. - (1986) A quantitative analysis of the behaviour of the Chinstrap and Macaroni Penguin on Bouvetoya during the late incubation and early nesting periods. *Polar Research,* 4: 33-46.

Handrich, Y. - (1989) Incubation water loss in King Penguin eggs. I. Change in egg and brood pouch parameters. *Physiological Zoology,* 62: 96-118.

Handrich, Y., Bevan, R.M., Charrassin, J.B., Butler, P.J., Pütz, K., Woakes, A.J., Lage, J. and Le Maho, Y. - (1997) Hypothermia in foraging King Penguins. *Nature*, 388: 64-67.

Harrison, P. - (1983) *Seabirds*. Croom Helm, Beckenham.

Hawkey, C.M., Horsley, D.T. and Keymer, I.F. - (1989) Haematology of wild penguins in the Falkland Islands. *Avian Pathology*, 18: 495-502.

Hays, C. - (1984) The Humboldt Penguin in Peru. *Oryx*, 18(2): 92-95.

Hays, C. - (1986) Effects of the 1982-83 El Niño on Humboldt Penguin colonies in Peru. *Biological Conservation*, 36: 169-180.

Herrero, R.I. - (1970) Informe privado sobre el número de nidos de (*Spheniscus magellanicus*) en Islas Tova y Tovita. Dirección de caza y conservación de la fauna. *Ministerio de Agricultura y Ganadería*. Buenos Aires.

Hindell, M.A. - (1988) The diet of the King Penguin at Macquarie Island. *Ibis*, 130: 193-203.

Hindell, M.A. - (1988) The diet of the Rockhopper Penguin at Macquarie Island. *Emu*, 88: 227-233.

Hindell, M.A. - (1989) The diet of Gentoo Penguins at Macquarie Island: winter and early breeding season. *Emu*, 89: 71-78.

Horne, R.S.C. - (1985) Diet of Royal and Rockhopper Penguins at Macquarie Islands. *Emu*, 85: 150-156.

Howland, H.C. and Sivak, J.G. - (1984) Penguin vision in air and water. *Vision Research*, 24: 1905-1909.

Hull, C.L. and Wilson, J. - (1996) The impact of investigators on the breeding success of Royal Penguins and Rockhopper Penguins on Macquarie Island. *Polar Biology*, 16: 335-337.

Hui, C.A. - (1985) Manoeuvrability of the Humboldt Penguin during swimming. *Canadian Journal of Zoology,* 63: 2165-2167.

Humphrey, P., Peterson, R., Bridge, D. and Reynolds, P. - (1970) *Birds of Isla Grande (Tierra del Fuego).* Preliminary manual. Smithsonian Institute, Washington DC.

Hunter, S. (1991) The impact of avian predator-scavengers on King Penguin chicks at Marion Island. *Ibis,* 133: 343-350.

Jablonski, B. - (1985) The diet of penguins on King George Island, South Shetland Islands. *Acta Zoologica Cracoviensia,* 29: 117-186.

Jackson, M. H. - (1985) *Galapagos: A Natural History Guide.* University of Calgary Press, Canada. 127pp.

Jehl, J.R. - (1975) Mortality of Magellanic Penguins in Argentina. *Auk,* 92: 596-598.

Jehl, J.R., Rumboll, M.A.E. and Winter, J.P. - (1973) Winter bird populations of Golfo San Jose, Argentina. *Bulletin of the British Ornithologists Club,* 93: 56-63.

Jenkins, R.J.F. - (1974) A new giant penguin from the Eocene of Australia. *Palaeontology,* 17: 291-310.

Jenkins, S.H. - (1978) Oil pollution in Argentina. *Marine Pollution Bulletin,* 14: 146-147.

Jerez, M. and Arancibia, P. - (1972) Trazado de isoyetas del sector centro oriental de la provincia de Magallanes. *Informe Instituto de la Patagonia,* Punta Arenas, Chile.

Johnson, A.W. - (1965) *The Birds of Chile,* Volume 1. Platt, Buenos Aires.

Johnson, K., Bednarz, J.C. and Zack, S. - (1987) Crested penguins: why are first eggs smaller? *Oikos,* 49: 347-349.

Jouventin, P. and Lagarde, R. - (1996) Evolutionary ecology of the King Penguin: the self-regulation of the breeding cycle. In *Penguin* biology: advances in research and management, (ed. P. Dann, I. Norman and P. Reilly), Surrey Beatty and Sons, Chipping Norton, Australia.

Jouventin, P and Mauget, R. - (1996) The endocrine basis of the reproductive cycle in the King Penguin. *Journal of Zoology, London.*

Jouventin, P., Capdeville, D., Cuenot-Chaillet, F. and Boiteau, C. - (1994) Exploitation of pelagic resources by a non-flying seabird: satellite-tracking of the King Penguin throughout the breeding cycle. *Marine Ecology Progress Series,* 106: 11-19.

Kato, A., Williams, T.D., Barton, T.R. and Rodwell, S. (1991) Short-term variation in the winter diet of Gentoo Penguins at South Georgia during July 1989. *Marine Ornithology,* 19: 31-38.

Keymer, I.F. - (1988) An investigation of Rockhopper Penguin mortality in the Falklands during the 1985-1986 breeding season. *Falkland Islands Foundation Project Report.*

Klages, N., Brooke, M. de L. and Watkins, B.P. - (1988) Prey of Rockhopper Penguins at Gough Island, South Atlantic Ocean. *Ostrich,* 59: 162-165.

Klages, N.T.W., Gales, R.P. and Pemberton, D. - (1989) Dietary segregation of Macaroni and Rockhopper Penguins at Heard Island. *Australian Wildlife Research,* 16: 599-604.

Klages, N.T.W., Pemberton, D. and Gales, R.P. - (1990) The diets of King and Gentoo Penguins at Heard Island. *Australian Wildlife Research,* 17: 53-60.

Knaus, R.M. - (1990) Estimates of oil-soaked carcasses of the Magellanic Penguin on the eastern shore of the Península Valdés, Argentina. *Hornero,* 13: 171-173.

Kooyman, G.L. - (1989) *Diverse divers.* Springer-Verlag, Berlin.

Kooyman, G.L. and Ponganis, P.J. - (1990) Behaviour and physiology of diving in Emperor and King Penguins. In *Penguin biology,* (ed. L.S. Davis and J.T. Darby), 229-242. Academic Press, San Diego.

Kooyman, G.L., Gentry, R.L., Bergman, W.P. and Hammel, H.T. - (1976) Heat loss in penguins during immersion and compression. *Comparative Biochemistry and Physiology,* 54A: 75-80.

Kooyman, G.L., Davis, R.W., Croxall, J.P. and Costa, D.P. - (1982) Diving depths and energy requirements of King Penguins. *Science,* 217: 726-727.

Kooyman, G.L., Cherel, Y., Le Maho, Y., Croxall, J.P., Thorson, P.H. and Ridoux, V. - (1992) Diving behaviour and energetics during foraging cycles in King Penguins. *Ecological Monographs,* 62: 143-163.

Lack, D. - (1968) *Ecological adaptations for breeding in birds.* Methuen, London.

La Cock, G.D., Hecht, T. and Klages, N. - (1984) The winter diet of Gentoo Penguins at Marion Island. *Ostrich,* 55: 188-191.

Lamey, T.C. - (1990) Hatching asynchrony and brood reduction in penguins. In *Penguin biology,* (ed. L.S. Davis and J.T. Darby), 399-416. Academic Press, San Diego.

Lamey, T.C. - (1993) Territorial aggression, timing of egg loss, and egg-size differences in Rockhopper Penguins on New Island, Falkland Islands. *Oikos,* 66:293-297.

Le Maho, Y., Gendner, J., Challet, E., Bost, C.A., Gilles, J., Verdon, C. Plumeré, C., Robin, J.P. and Handrich, Y. - (1993) Undisturbed breeding penguins as indicators of changes in marine resources. *Marine Ecology Progress Series,* 95: 1-6.

Le Maho, Y., Robin, J.P. and Cherel, Y. - (1988) Starvation as a treatment for obesity: the need to conserve body protein. *News in Physical Sciences,* 3: 21-24.

Lenfant, C., Kooyman, G.L., Elsner, R. and Drabek, C.M. - (1969) Respiratory function of the blood of the Adelie Penguin. *American Journal of Physiology,* 216: 1598-1600.

Le Ninan, F., Cherel, Y., Robin, J.P., Leloup, J., and Le Maho, Y. - (1988) Early changes in plasma hormones and metabolites during fasting in King Penguin chicks. *Journal of Comparative Physiology B,* 158: 395-401.

Le Ninan, F., Cherel, Y., Sardet, C. and Le Maho, Y. - (1988) Plasma hormone levels in relation to lipid and protein metabolism during prolonged fasting in King Penguin chicks. *General and Comparative Endocrinology,* 71: 331-337.

Lewis Smith, R.I. and Tallowin, J.R.B. - (1979) The distribution and size of King Penguin rookeries on South Georgia. *British Antarctic Survey Bulletin* 49: 259-276.

Lewis Smith, R.I. and Prince, P.A. - (1985) The natural history of Beauchene Island, Falkland Islands. *Biological Journal of the Linnean Society,* 24: 233-283.

Livezey, B.C. - (1989) Morphometric patterns in recent and fossil penguins *(Aves Sphenisciformes). Journal of Zoology*, London. 219: 269-307.

Martin, G. - (1985) Through a penguin's eye. *New Scientist,* 14/3: 29-31

Mauget, R., Jouventin, P., Lacroix, A. and Ishii, S. - (1994) Plasma LH and steroid hormones in King Penguin during the onset of the breeding cycle. *General and Comparative Endocrinology,* 93: 36-43.

Merritt, K. and King, N.E. - (1987) Behavioural sex differences and activity patterns of captive Humboldt Penguins. *Zoo Biology,* 6: 129-138.

Moore, G.J. and Robertson, G.G. - (1993) Population parameters of the King Penguin at Heard Island over the 1992 and 1993 breeding seasons: population size, patterns of chick mortality, fledging patterns and morphometrics. In *Heard Island 1992 ANARE Report.* Australian Antarctic Division, Tasmania.

Moors, P.J. - (1986) Decline in numbers of Rockhopper Penguins at Campbell Island. *Polar Record,* 23: 69-73.

Mougin, J.L. - (1984) La ponte du gorfou macaroni, *Eudyptes chrysolophus,* de l'Archipel Crozet. *L'Oiseau et la Revue Francaise d'Ornithologie,* 54: 281-291.

Mougin, J.L. and Prevost, J. - (1980) Evolution annuelle des effectifs et des biomasses des oiseaux antarctiques. *Terre et Vie,* 34: 101-133.

Müller-Schwarze, D. and Müller-Schwarze, C. - (1980) Display rate and speed of nest-relief in Antarctic *Pygoscelid* penguins. *Auk,* 97: 825-831.

Murphy, R.C. - (1936) *Oceanic birds of South America,* American Museum of Natural History, New York.

Murray, M.D. - (1964) Ecology of the ectoparasites of seals and penguins. In *Antarctic biology,* (ed. R. Carrick, M. Holdgate and J. Prévost), 241-245, Hermann. Paris.

Murrish, D.E. - (1973) Respiratory heat and water exchange in penguins. *Respiratory Physiology,* 19: 262-270.

Napier, R.B. (1968) Erect-crested and Rockhopper Penguins interbreeding in the Falkland Islands. *British Antarctic Survey Bulletin,* 16: 71-72.

Navarro, J. and Pequeño, G. - (1979) Peces litorales de los Archipiélagos de Chiloé y Los Chonos, Chile. *Revue de Biologia Marina,* 16(3): 255-309.

O'Hara, R.L. - (1989) An estimate of the phylogeny of the living penguins. *American Zoologist,* 29: 11A.

Oliver, W.R.B. - (1953) The crested penguins of New Zealand. *Emu*, 53: 185-187.

Olrog, C.C. - (1950) Mamíferos y Aves del Archipiélago de Cabo de Hornos. *Acta Zoológica Lilloana*, 9: 505-532.

Olrog, O.O. - (1979) Nueva Lista de la Avifauna Argentina. *Acta Zoológica Lilloana*, 27.

Olson, S.L. and Hasegawa, Y. - (1979) Fossil counterparts of giant penguins from the North Pacific. *Science*, 206: 688-689.

Olsson, C.O. - (1995) *Timing and body-reserve adjustment in King Penguin reproduction*. Unpublished thesis, University of Uppsala.

Olsson, C.O. - (1996) Seasonal effects of timing and reproduction in the King Penguin: a unique breeding cycle. *Journal of Avian Biology*, 27: 7-14.

Olsson, C.O. and North A.W. - (1997) Diet of the King Penguin during three summers at South Georgia. *Ibis*.

Oustalet, E. - (1991) Oiseaux. *Mission Scientifique du Cap Horn 1882-1883*. Zoologie 6: 1-341.

Pagnoni, G., Perez, D. and Bertellotti, M. - (1993) Distribución, abundancia y densidad de nidos en Isla de los Pájaros, Chubut, Argentina. *Jornadas Nacionales de Ciencias del Mar*.

Paredes, R. and Zavalaga, C.B. - (1998) Overview of the effects of El Niño 1997-98 on Humboldt Penguins and other seabirds at Punta San Juan, Peru. *Penguin Conservation*, 11(1): 5-7.

Pequeño, G. - (1986) Comments on fishes from the Diego Ramirez Islands, Chile. *Japanese Journal of Ichthyology*, 32(4): 440-442.

Perkins, J.S. - (1983) Oiled Magellanic Penguins in Golfo San José, Argentina. *Marine Pollution Bulletin*, 14: 383-387.

Perkins, J.S. - (1984) Breeding ecology of Magellanic Penguins at Caleta Valdés, Argentina. *Cormorant,* 12: 3-13.

Pettingill, O.S. - (1960) Creche behaviour and individual recognition in a colony of Rockhopper Penguins. *Wilson Bulletin,* 72: 213-221.

Philander, G. - (1989) El Niño and La Niña. *American Scientist 77,* 5: 451-459.

Pinshow, B., Fedak, M.A. and Schmidt-Nielson, K. - (1977) Terrestrial locomotion in penguins: it costs more to waddle. *Science,* 195: 592-594.

Pisano, E. - (1971) Estudio Ecológico Preliminar del Parque Nacional Los Pingüinos (Estrecho de Magallanes). *Anales del Instituto de la Patagonia,* 2: 76-92. Punta Arenas, Chile.

Pisano, V.E. - (1972) Observaciones fitoecológicas en las islas Diego Ramirez. *Anales del Instituto de la Patagonia,* 3: 161-169. Punta Arenas, Chile.

Pisano, V.E. - (1980) Catálogo de la flora vascular del archipiélago del Cabo de Hornos. *Anales del Instituto de la Patagonia,* 11: 151-189. Punta Arenas, Chile.

Pisano, V.E. and Schlatter, R.P. - (1981) Vegetación y flora de las islas Diego Ramirez (Chile). I. Características y relaciones de su flora vascular. *Anales del Instituto de la Patagonia,* 12: 183-194. Punta Arenas, Chile.

Pisano, V.E. and Schlatter, R.P. - (1981) Vegetación y flora de las islas Diego Ramirez (Chile). II. - Comunidades vegetales vasculares. *Anales del Instituto de la Patagonia,* 12: 195-204. Punta Arenas, Chile.

Punta, G. - (1989) Guaneras de la provincia del Chubut. Potencialidad productiva y fundamentos para su manejo racional. *Dir. Imp. Of.* Rawson.

Pütz, K. - (1994) Aspects of the feeding ecology of Emperor Penguins and King Penguins. *Report Polar Research,* 136: 1-139.

Pütz, K. - (1994) Untersuchungen zur Ernahrungsokologie von Kaiserpinguinen (*Aptenodytes forsteri*) und Konigspinguinen (*Aptenodytes patagonicus*). *Ber Polarforsch,* 136: 1-139.

Pütz, K. and Bost, C.A. - (1994) Feeding behaviour of free-ranging King Penguins. *Ecology,* 75: 489-497.

Raikow, R.J., Bicanovsky, L. and Bledsoe, A.H. - (1988) Forelimb and joint mobility and the evolution of wing-propelled diving in birds. *Auk,* 105: 446-451.

Regel, J. and Pütz, K. - (1997) Effect of human disturbance on body temperature and energy expenditure in penguins. *Polar Biology,* 18: 246-253.

Reid, W.V. and Boersma, P.D. - (1990) Parental quality and selection on egg size in the Magellanic Penguin. *Evolution,* 44: 1780-1786.

Reilly, P. - (1994) *Penguins of the World.* Oxford University Press, London.

Reilly, P.N. and Kerle, J.A. - (1981) A study of the Gentoo Penguin. *Notornis,* 28: 189-202.

Reynolds, P.W. - (1935) Notes on the birds of Cape Horn. *Ibis Series 13,* 5: 65-101.

Richdale, L.E. - (1957) *A population study of penguins.* Oxford University Press, London.

Roberts, B.B. - (1940) The breeding behaviour of penguins. In *British Graham Land Expedition 1934-1937,* Science Report 1, 195-254.

Robertson, G. - (1986) Population size and breeding success of the Gentoo Penguin at Macquarie Island. *Australian Wildlife Research.* 13: 583-587.

Robertson, G. - (1990) Huddles. *Australian Geographic*, 20: 74-97.

Rosenberg, D.K., Valle, C.A., Coulter, M.C. and Harcourt, S.A. - (1990) Monitoring Galapagos penguins and flightless cormorants in the Galapagos Islands. *Wilson Bulletin*, 102: 525-532.

Rounsevell, D.E. and Copson, G.R. - (1982) Growth rate and recovery of a King Penguin population after exploitation. *Australian Wildlife Research*, 9: 519-525.

Ryan, P.G. and Cooper, J. - (1991) Rockhopper Penguins and other marine life threatened by drift-net fisheries at Tristan de Cunha. *Oryx*, 25: 76-79.

SCAR. - (1996) Status and trends of Antarctic and sub-Antarctic seabirds. *Report of the Fifteenth Meeting of the Scientific Committee of CCAMLR.* Hobart.

Schlatter, R.P. - (1984) The status and conservation of seabirds in Chile. In *Status and conservation of the world's seabirds*, ICBP Technical Publication No.2, (ed. J.P. Croxall, P.G.H. Evans and R.W. Schreiber), 261-269. ICBP, Cambridge.

Schlatter, R.P. and Riveros, G.M. - (1984) Number of seabirds at the Diego Ramirez Islands. Unpublished report.

Scholten, C.J. - (1987) Breeding biology of the Humboldt Penguin at Emmen Zoo. *International Zoo Yearbook*, 26: 198-204.

Scholten, C.J. - (1989) Individual recognition of Humboldt Penguins. *Spheniscid Penguin Newsletter*, 2: 4-8.

Scholten, C.J. - (1989) The timing of moult in relation to age, sex and breeding status in a group of captive Humboldt Penguin at Emmen Zoo, The Netherlands. *Netherlands Journal of Zoology*, 39: 113-125.

Scholten, C.J. - (1991) Research on seabirds in captivity: a contradicto in terminis. *Sula*, 5: 41-49.

Scholten, C.J. - (1992) Choice of nest-site and mate in Humboldt Penguins. *Spheniscid Penguin Newsletter,* 5: 3-13.

Scolaro, J.A. - (1980) El pingüino de Magellanes *(Spheniscus magellanicus)* VI. Dinamica de la población de juveniles. *Historia Natural,* 1: 173-178.

Scolaro, J.A. - (1983) The ecology of the Magellanic Penguin. A long-term population and breeding study of a temperate latitude penguin in Southern Argentina. Unpublished thesis, University of Bradford, England.

Scolaro, J.A. - (1984) Timing of nest relief during incubation and guard stage period of chicks in Magellanic Penguin. *Historia Natural,* 4: 281-284.

Scolaro, J.A. - (1984) Madurez sexual del pingüino de Magellanes (*Spheniscus magellanicus*). *Historia Natural,* 4: 289-292.

Scolaro, J.A. - (1986) La conservación del pingüino de Magellanes: una problema de conflicto e intereses que requiere de argumentos cientificos. *Anales del Museo de Historia Natural de Valparaiso,* 17: 113-119.

Scolaro, J.A. - (1990) Effects of nest density on breeding success in a colony of Magellanic Penguins. *Colonial Waterbirds,* 13: 41-49.

Scolaro, J.A. and Badano, L.A. - (1986) Diet of the Magellanic Penguin during the chick-rearing period at Punta Clara, Argentina. *Cormorant,* 13: 91-97.

Scolaro, J.A. and Suburo, A.M. - (1991) Maximum diving depths of the Magellanic Penguin. *Journal of Field Ornithology,* 62: 204-210.

Scolaro, J.A., Rodriguez, E.N. and Monochio, A.A. - (1980) El Pingüino de Magallanes. V Distribución de las colonias de reproducción en el territorio continental Argentino. *Ciencias Nacionales, Patagonia Contribuciones,* 33: 1-18.

Scolaro, J.A., Badano, L.A. and Upton, J.A. - (1984) Estimación de la población y estructura de la nidificación de *Spheniscus magellanicus* en Punta Loberia, Chubut, Argentina. *Historia Natural,* 4: 229-238.

Simeone, A. - (1998) Ecology and Conservation of penguins in Chile: a symposium. *Penguin Conservation,* 11(1): 16-24.

Sivak, J.G. - (1976) The role of a flat cornea in the amphibious behaviour of the Blackfoot Penguin. *Canadian Journal of Zoology,* 54: 1341-1345.

Sivak, J.G., Howland, H.C. and McGill-Harelstad, P. - (1987) Vision of the Humboldt Penguin in air and water. *Proceedings of the Royal Society of London, Series B,* 229: 467-472.

Sladen, W.J.L. - (1954) Penguins in the wild and in captivity. *Aviculture Magazine,* 60: 132-142.

Sladen, W.J.L. - (1958) The *Pygoscelis* penguins. 1. Methods of study. 2. The Adelie Penguin. *Falkland Islands Dependency Survey Science Report,* 17: 1-97.

Smith, R.I.L. and Prince, P.A. - (1985) The natural history of Beauchene Island. *Biological Journal of the Linnean Society,* 24: 233-283.

Soto, N. - (1990) Proyecto de proteccion y manejo de las colonias de pingüinos presentes en Isla Rupert e Isla Recalada Reserva Nacional Alacalufes. *Informe de Temporada 1989-1990,* CONAF XII Región, Punta Arenas.

St. Clair, C.C. - (1996) Multiple mechanisms of reversed hatching asynchrony in Rockhopper Penguins. *Journal of Animal Ecology,* 65: 485-494.

St. Clair, C.C. and St. Clair, R.C. - (1996) Causes and consequences of egg loss in Rockhopper Penguins. *Oikos.*

Splettstoesser, J.F. - (1985) Note on rock striations caused by penguin feet, Falkland Islands. *Arctic and Alpine Research.* 17: 107-111.

Stahl, J.C., Derenne, P., Jouventin, P., Mougin, J.L., Teulieres, L. and Weimerskirch, H. - (1985) Le cycle reproducteur des gorfous de l'archipel Crozet: *Eudyptes chrysolophus,* le gorfou macaroni et *Eudyptes chrysocome,* le gorfou sauteur. *L'Oiseau et la Revue Francaise d'Ornithologie.* 55: 27-43.

Stokes, D.L. - (1994) Nesting habitat use, value and selection in Magellanic Penguins. Unpublished thesis. University of Washington, Seattle.

Stokes, D.L. and Boersma, P.D. - (1991) Effects of substrate on the distribution of Magellanic Penguin burrows. *Auk,* 108: 923-933.

Stonehouse, B. - (1960) The King Penguin of South Georgia I. Breeding behaviour and development. *Scientific Report of the Falkland Islands Dependency Survey,* 23: 1-81.

Stonehouse, B. - (1969) Environmental temperatures of tertiary penguins. *Science,* 163: 673-675.

Stonehouse, B. - (1970) Geographic variation in Gentoo Penguins. *Ibis,* 112: 52-57.

Strange, I.J. - (1982) Breeding ecology of the Rockhopper Penguin in the Falkland Islands. *Le Gerfaut,* 72: 137-187.

Strange, I.J. - (1992) *Field Guide to the wildlife of the Falkland Islands and South Georgia.* HarperCollins, London.

Taylor, J.R.E. - (1986) Thermal insulation of the down and feathers of *Pygoscelid* penguin chicks and the unique properties of penguin feathers. *Auk,* 103: 160-168.

Taylor, R. and Wilson, P. - (1982) Counting Antarctic penguins from the air. *Antarctic,* 9: 366-368.

Thompson, K.R. - (1989) An assessment of the potential for competition between seabirds and fisheries in the Falkland Islands. *Falkland Islands Foundation Project Report.*

Thompson, K.R. - (1989) Seabird research undertaken on Steeple Jason Island, Falkland Islands, in the austral summer of 1987/88. *Falkland Islands Foundation Project Report.*

Thompson, K.R. - (1992) Intersite variation in Magellanic Penguin diet in the Falkland Islands: implications for monitoring. *Corella,* 16: 151.

Thompson, K.R. - (1994) Predation on *Gonatus antarcticus* by Falkland Islands seabirds. *Antarctic Science,* 6: 269-274.

Tovar, H. and Cabrera, D. - (1985) Las Aves Gunaeras y el Fenomeno El Niño. In *El Niño.* (ed. W. Arntz, A. Landa and J. Tarazona), 181-186. Bolivian Marine Institute, Peru-Callao.

Trawa, G. - (1970) Note préliminaire sur la vascularisation des membres des *Spheniscides* de Terre Adélie. *L'Oiseau et la Revue Francaise d'Ornithologie,* 40: 142-156.

Trivelpiece, S.G., Trivelpiece, W.Z. and Volkman, N.J. - (1985) Plumage characteristics of juvenile *Pygoscelid* penguins. *Ibis,* 127: 378-380.

Trivelpiece, W.Z. and Trivelpiece, S.G. - (1990) Courtship period of Adelie, Gentoo and Chinstrap Penguins. In *Penguin biology,* (ed. L.S. Davis and J.T. Darby), 113-127. Academic Press, San Diego.

Trivelpiece, W.Z., Trivelpiece, S.G., Volkman, N.J. and Ware, S.H. - (1983) Breeding and feeding ecology of *Pygoscelid* penguins. *Antarctic Journal of the United States,* 18: 209-210.

Trivelpiece, W.Z., Bengtson, J.L., Trivelpiece, S.G. and Volkman, N.J. - (1986) Foraging behaviour of Gentoo and Chinstrap Penguins as determined by new radio-telemetry techniques. *Auk,* 103: 777-781.

Trivelpiece, W.Z., Trivelpiece, S.G. and Volkman, N.J. - (1987) Ecological segregation of Adelie, Gentoo and Chinstrap Penguins at King George Island, Antarctica. *Ecology,* 68: 351-361.

Trivers, R.L. - (1974) Parent-offspring conflict. *American Zoology,* 14: 249-264.

Valle, C.A. and Coulter, M.C. - (1987) Present status of the Flightless Cormorant, Galapagos Penguin and Greater Flamingo populations in the Galapagos Islands, Ecuador, after the 1982-83 El Niño. *Condor,* 89: 276-281.

Valle, C.A., Cruz, F., Cruz, J.B., Merlen, G. and Coulter, M.C. - (1987) The impact of the 1982-83 El Niño Southern Oscillation on seabirds in the Galapagos Islands, Ecuador. *Journal of Geophysical Research,* 92: 14437-14444.

van Heezik, Y.M., Seddon, P.J., du Plessis, C.J. and Adams, N.J. - (1993) Differential growth of King Penguin chicks in relation to date of hatching. *Colonial Waterbirds,* 16: 71-76.

van Heezik, Y.M., Seddon, P.J., Cooper, J. and Plos, A. - (1994) Interrelationships between breeding frequency, timing and outcome in King Penguins: are King Penguins biennial breeders? *Ibis,* 136: 279-284.

van Zinderen Bakker, E.M.Jr. - (1971) A behavioural analysis of the Gentoo Penguin. In *Marion and Prince Edward Islands, Republic of South Africa biological and geological expedition 1965-1966,* (ed. E. van Zinderen Bakker Sr., J.M. Winterbottom and R.A. Dyer), 251-272. Balkema, Capetown.

Vargas, H. - (1996) Galapagos Penguin Census of 1995. *Penguin Conservation,* Vol.9 No.1: 2-4.

Venegas, C. - (1978) Pingüinos de barbijo *(Pygoscelis antarctica)* y macaroni *(Eudyptes chrysolophus)* en Magallanes. *Anales del Instituto de la Patagonia,* 9: 179-189.

Venegas, C. - (1981) Aves de las islas Wollaston y Bayly, en el Archipiélago del Cabo de Hornos. *Anales Instituto de la Patagonia,* 12: 213-219.

Venegas, C. - (1982) Nuevos registros ornithológicas en Magallanes. *Anales del Instituto de la Patagonia,* 13: 173-187.

Venegas, C. - (1982) Aves de la isla Grevy. In: Investigación y Experimentación de Recursos Natura-les en el Archipiélago del Cabo de Hornos. *Informe Instituto de la Patagonia,* 11: 68-80.

Venegas, C. - (1984) Estado de las poblaciones de Pingüino de Penacho Amarillo y Macaroni en la Isla Noir, Chile. *Informe Instituto de la Patagonia,* 33.

Venegas, C. - (1984) Estudios Ornitológicos Subantárticos en Isla Noir. *Informe al Consejo Superior de Ciencia del Proyecto 104/82.*

Venegas, C. - (1986) *Aves de Patagonia y Tierra del Fuego Chileno-Argentina.* Ediciones de la Universidad de Magallanes, Punta Arenas.

Venegas, C. - (1991) Ensambles avifaunisticos estivales del Archipiélago Cabo de Hornos. *Anales del Instituto de la Patagonia,* 20(1): 69-82.

Venegas, C. - (1991) Estudio de cuantificacion poblacional de pingüinos crestados en Isla Recalada. *Informe Instituto de la Patagonia,* 55.

Venegas, C. - (1994) *Aves de Magallanes.* Ediciones de la Universidad de Magallanes, Punta Arenas.

Venegas, C. and Sielfeld, K.W. - (1979) Antecedentes para la determinación de un nuevo distrito zoogeografico en el litoral exterior de Magallanes. *Anales del Instituto de la Patagonia,* 10: 201-208.

Venegas, C and Sielfeld, W. - (1981) Utilización de aves como indicadoras de presencia y potencialidad de recursos marinos eventualmente manejables. In *Jornadas Ciencias del Mar,* Universidad de Valparaíso.

Viot, C.R. - (1987) Différenciation et isolement entre populations chez le manchot royal *(Aptenodytes patagonicus)* et le manchot papou *(Pygoscelis papua)* des Iles Crozet et Kerguelen. *L'Oiseau et la Revue Francaise d'Ornithologie,* 57: 251-259.

Voisin, J.F. - (1971) Note sur les manchots royaux *(Aptenodytes patagonica)* de l'ile de la Possession. *L'Oiseau et la Revue Francaise d'Ornithologie,* 41: 176-180.

Volkman, N.J. and Trivelpiece, W. - (1980) Growth of *Pygoscelid* penguin chicks. *Journal of Zoology, London,* 191: 521-530.

Volkman, N.J. and Trivelpiece, W. - (1981) Nest site selection among Adelie, Chinstrap and Gentoo Penguins in mixed species rookeries. *Wilson Bulletin,* 93: 243-248.

Volkman, N.J., Presler, P. and Trivelpiece, W. - (1980) Diets of *Pygoscelid* penguins at King George Island, Antarctica. *Condor,* 82: 373-378.

Volkman, N.J., Trivelpiece, S.G., Trivelpiece, W.Z. and Young, K.E. - (1982) Comparative studies of *Pygoscelid* penguins in Admiralty Bay. *Antarctic Journal of the United States,* 17: 180.

Waas, J.R. - (1995) Social stimulation and reproductive schedules: does the acoustic environment influence the egg-laying schedule in penguin colonies? In *Penguin biology: Advances in research and management.* (ed. P. Dann, I. Norman and P. Reilly). Surrey Beatty, Australia.

Warham, J. - (1963) The Rockhopper Penguin at Macquarie Island. *Auk,* 80: 229-256.

Warham, J. - (1972) Breeding season and sexual dimorphism in Rockhopper Penguins. *Auk,* 89: 86-105.

Warham, J. - (1973) Breeding biology and behaviour of the *Eudyptes* penguins. Unpublished thesis. University of Canterbury, New Zealand.

Warham, J. - (1975) The crested penguins. In *The biology of penguins,* (ed. B. Stonehouse), 189-269. Macmillan, London.

Weimerskirch, H., Stahl, J.C. and Jouventin, P. - (1992) The breeding biology and population dynamics of King Penguins on the Crozet Islands. *Ibis,* 134: 107-117.

White, M.G. and Conroy, J.W.H. - (1975) Aspects of competition between *Pygoscelid* penguins at Signy Island, South Orkney Islands. *Ibis,* 117: 371-373.

Williams, A.J. - (1980) Offspring reduction in Macaroni and Rockhopper Penguins. *Auk,* 97: 754-759.

Williams, A.J. - (1980) Aspects of the breeding biology of the Gentoo penguin. *Le Gerfaut,* 70: 283-295.

Williams, A.J. - (1980) Rockhopper Penguins at Gough Island. *Bulletin of the British Ornithological Club,* 100: 208-212.

Williams, A.J. - (1981) The clutch size of Macaroni and Rockhopper Penguins. *Emu,* 81: 87-90.

Williams, A.J. - (1981) Why do penguins have long laying intervals? *Ibis,* 123: 202-204.

Williams, A.J. - (1981) Factors affecting time of breeding of Gentoo Penguin at Marion Island. In *Proceedings of the symposium on birds of the sea and shore 1979,* (ed. J. Cooper), 451-459. African Seabird Group, Capetown.

Williams, A.J. - (1981) The laying interval and incubation period of Rockhopper and Macaroni Penguins. *Ostrich,* 52: 226-229.

Williams, A.J. - (1982) Chick-feeding rates of Macaroni and Rockhopper Penguins at Marion Island. *Ostrich,* 53: 129-134.

Williams, A.J. and Siegfried, W.R. - (1980) Foraging ranges of krill-eating penguins. *Polar Record,* 20: 159-162.

Williams, A.J. and Stone, C. - (1981) Rockhopper Penguins at Tristan da Cunha. *Cormorant,* 9: 59-65.

Williams, A.J., Siegfried, W.R., Burger, A.E. and Berruti, A. - (1977) Body composition and energy metabolism of moulting *Eudyptid* penguins. *Comparative Biochemistry and Physiology,* 56A: 27-30.

Williams, A.J., Siegfried, W.R. and Cooper, J. - (1982) Egg composition and hatchling precocity in seabirds. *Ibis,* 124: 456-470.

Williams, A.J., Cooper, J., Newton, I.P., Phillips, C.M. and Watkins, B.P. - (1985) *Penguins of the world: a bibliography.* British Antarctic Survey, Cambridge.

Williams, T.D. - (1988) Plumage characteristics of juvenile and adult Gentoo Penguins. *Ibis,* 130: 565-566.

Williams, T.D. - (1989) Aggression, incubation behaviour and egg loss in Macaroni Penguins at South Georgia. *Oikos,* 55: 19-22.

Williams, T.D. - (1990) Growth and survival in Macaroni Penguin A- and B- chicks: do females maximise investment in the large B-egg? *Oikos,* 59: 349-354.

Williams, T.D. - (1990) Annual variation in breeding biology of the Gentoo Penguins at Bird Island, South Georgia. *Journal of Zoology, London.* 222: 247-258.

Williams, T.D. - (1991) Foraging ecology and diet of Gentoo Penguins at South Georgia during winter and an assessment of their winter prey consumption. *Ibis,* 133: 3-13.

Williams, T.D. - (1992) Reproductive endocrinology of Macaroni and Gentoo Penguins I. Seasonal changes in plasma levels of gonadal steroids and LH in breeding adults. *General and Comparative Endocrinology,* 85: 230-240.

Williams, T.D. - (1992) Reproductive endocrinology of Macaroni and Gentoo Penguins II. Plasma levels of gonadal steroids and LH in immature birds in relation to deferred sexual maturity. *General and Comparative Endocrinology,* 85: 241-247.

Williams, T.D. and Croxall, J.P. - (1990) Is chick fledging weight a good index of food availability in seabird populations? *Oikos,* 59: 414-416.

Williams, T.D. and Croxall, J.P. - (1991) Chick growth and survival in Gentoo Penguins: effect of hatching asynchrony and variation in food supply. *Polar Biology,* 11: 197-202.

Williams, T.D. and Croxall, J.P. - (1991) Annual variation in breeding biology of Macaroni Penguins at Bird Island, South Georgia. *Journal of Zoology, London,* 223: 189-202.

Williams, T.D. and Rodwell, S. - (1992) Annual variation in return rate, mate and nest-site fidelity in breeding Gentoo and Macaroni Penguins. *Condor,* 94: 636-645.

Williams, T.D. and Rothery, P. - (1990) Factors affecting variation in foraging and activity patterns of Gentoo Penguins during the breeding season at Bird Island, South Georgia. *Journal of Applied Ecology,* 27: 1042-1054.

Williams, T.D., Briggs, D.R., Croxall, J.P., Naito, Y. and Kato, A. - (1992) Diving pattern and performance in relation to foraging ecology in the Gentoo Penguin. *Journal of Zoology, London,* 227: 211-230.

Williams, T.D., Kato, A., Croxall, J.P., Naito, Y., Briggs, D.R., Rodwell, S. *et al.* - (1992) Diving pattern and performances in non-breeding Gentoo Penguins during winter. *Auk,* 109: 223-234.

Williams, T.D., Ghebremeskel, K., Williams, G. and Crawford, M.A. - (1992) Breeding and moulting fasts in Macaroni Penguins: do birds exhaust their fat reserves? *Comparative Biochemistry and Physiology,* 103A: 783-785.

Williams *et al.* - (1989) Plasma a-tocopherol, total lipids and total cholesterol in wild Rockhopper, Magellanic and Gentoo penguins before and after moulting. *Veterinary Rec.* 124: 585-586.

Wilson, R.P. - (1989) Diving depths of Gentoo and Adelie Penguins at Esperanza Bay, Antarctic Peninsula. *Cormorant,* 17:1-8.

Wilson, R.P. - (1997) A restraint method for penguins. *Marine Ornithology.*

Wilson, R.P. and Wilson, M.P.T. - (1989) Substitute burrows for penguins on guano-free islands. *Gerfaut,* 79: 125-132.

Wilson, R.P. and Wilson, M.P. - (1990) Foraging ecology of breeding *Spheniscus* penguins. In *Penguin biology,* (ed. L.S. Davis and J.T. Darby), 181-206. Academic Press, San Diego.

Wilson, R.P., Grant, W.S. and Duffy, D.C. - (1986) Recording devices on free-ranging marine animals: does measurement affect foraging performance? *Ecology,* 67: 1091-1093.

Wilson, R.P., Ryan, P.G., James, A. and Wilson, M.P. - (1987) Conspicuous coloration may enhance prey capture in some piscivores. *Animal Behaviour,* 35: 1558-1560.

Wilson, R.P., Wilson, M.P., Duffy, D.C., Araya, B. and Klages, N. - (1989) Diving behaviour and prey of the Humboldt Penguin. *Journal für Ornithologie,* 10: 75-79.

Wilson, R.P., Cooper, J. and Pütz, K. - (1992) Can we determine when marine endotherms feed? A case study with seabirds. *Journal of Experimental Biology,* 167: 267-275.

Wilson, R.P., Pütz, K., Bost, C.A., Culik, B.M., Bannasch, R., Reins, T. *et al.* - (1993) Diel dive depth in penguins in relation to diel vertical migration of prey: whose dinner by candlelight? *Marine Ecology Progress Series,* 94: 101-104.

Wilson, R.P., Pütz, K., Peters, G., Culik ,B., Scolaro, A.J., Charrassin, J.B. and Ropert-Coudert, Y. - (1997) Long-term attachment of transmitting and recording devices to penguins and other seabirds. *Wildlife Society Bulletin,* 25.

Woehler, E.J. - (1993) *The Distribution and Abundance of Antarctic and Subantarctic Penguins.* SCAR, Cambridge.

Yorio, P.M. and Boersma, P.D. - (1992) The effects of human disturbance on Magellanic Penguin behaviour and breeding success. *Bird Conservation International,* 2: 161-173.

Yorio, P.M. and Boersma, P.D. - (1994) Consequences of nest desertion and inattendance for Magellanic Penguin hatching success. *Auk,* 111(1): 215-217.

Yorio, P.M., Quintana, F., Campagna, C. and Harris, G. - (1995) Diversidad, abundancia y dinámica espacio-temporal de la colonia mixta de aves marinas en Punta León, Patagonia. *Ornitología Neotropical.*

Zapata, A.R.P. - (1967) Observaciónes sobre aves de Puerto Deseado, provincia de Santa Cruz. *Hornero,* 10(4): 351-378.

Zavalaga, C.B. and Paredes, R. - (1997) Humboldt Penguins at Punta San Juan, Peru. *Penguin Conservation,* Vol.10 No.1: 6-8.

GLOSSARY

ALLOPREENING: the process whereby one bird preens another bird's plumage.

ANAEROBIC: in the absence of oxygen.

BIOLUMINOUS: describes living tissue which emits light.

BIOMASS: total weight of organic material.

CULMINICORN: side of the upper beak.

DECAPOD: crustacean with ten thoracic legs such as shrimps, lobsters, crayfish and crabs.

ECTOSKELETON: hard outer skin of invertebrates.

EGGING: local term for the taking of eggs for human consumption.

ENSO: abbreviation for El Niño Southern Oscillation. Refers to the process whereby cool nutrient rich waters which flow northwards along the coast of Chile and Peru, become displaced by warmer nutrient poor waters flowing from the central Pacific. This loss of nutrients is characterised by a slowing down of primary production by phytoplankton, which in turn leads to changes in the entire marine food chain.

FURCULA: one-piece collar bone found in birds.

MANDIBULAR PLATE: coloured patch running from the lower beak to the cheek.

MESOPTILE PLUMAGE: thick downy plumage of chicks.

PROTOPTILE PLUMAGE: very sparse plumage of very young chicks.

OCCIPITAL CREST: crest of erect feathers found around the head of certain penguins.

ORCA: killer whale

PINIPEDS: sea lions, seals and walruses.

UROPYGIAL GLAND: gland at the base of the tail that produces wax for waterproofing plumage.

Index

albatross: see Black-browed
Aptenodytes patagonicus: see King Penguin
Archaeopteryx lithographica: 3
Austroatherina sp.: 55
Black-browed Albatross: 39, 41
caracaras: 33, 45, 66, 75, 87
cats: 70
cetaceans: 66, 75
Champsocephalus gunneri: 51
Chionis alba: see Snowy Sheathbill
crabs: 70
detritivores: 76, 77
dogs: 66, 70
Dolphin Gull: 75
El Niño: see ENSO
Engraulis sp.: 55, 64, 66
ENSO: 15, 65, 66, 68, 69, 70, 88
Eudyptes chrysocome: see Rockhopper Penguin
Eudyptes chrysolophus: see Macaroni Penguin
Euphausia sp.: 41, 51
foxes: 66, 87
Fur Seal: 33, 70, 86
Galapagos Penguin: 19, 53, 67 - 71, 88
Gentoo Penguin: 8, 16, 25, 26, 27, 28, 29 - 37, 40, 46, 80, 83, 84
Gonatus antarcticus: 26, 32, 41, 51, 55
geese: 77
gulls: see Dolphin / Kelp
hawks: 70
Humboldt Penguin: 19, 36, 62 - 66, 79, 82, 88
Kelp Gull: 75
King Cormorant: 32, 41
King Penguin: 9, 10, 23 - 28, 86
Lanternfish: 9, 26

Larus dominicanus: see Kelp Gull
Larus scoresbii: see Dolphin Gull
Leopard Seal: 15, 27, 33, 59
Lobster Krill: see *Munida gregaria*
Loligo gahi: 32, 41, 51, 55
Macaroni Penguin: 8, 48 - 51
Magellanic Penguin: 8, 19, 27, 52 - 61, 63, 78, 79, 85, 88
Merluccius hubbsi: 55
Micromesistius australis: 32, 37
Moroteuthis ingens: 26, 32, 55
Munida gregaria: 32, 51, 55
Myxinus sp.: 55
Normanichthys crockeri: 64
Notothenia sp.: 51
Odonthestes regia: 64
Onychoteuthis sp.: 26, 41, 55
Orca: 15, 27, 33, 45, 51, 59
owls: 70
Palaeeudyptes antarcticus: 4
Parodiochloa flabellata: see Tussac Grass
Patagonia: 23, 79
Patagonotothen sp.: 32, 55
Phalacrocorax atriceps: see King Cormorant
phytoplankton: 65
pinipeds: 66, 75
Procellaria aequinoctialis: see White-chinned Petrel
Puffinus griseus: see Sooty Shearwater
Pygoscelis papua: see Gentoo Penguin
rabbits: 77
rats: 70
Rockhopper Penguin: 8, 9, 16, 38 - 47, 48, 49, 83, 84, 85, 86, 88
Sardinops sagax: 64
Scomberesox sp.: 64
Sea Lion: 15, 27, 33, 45, 51, 59, 70, 78, 86
Sheathbill: see Snowy
sharks: 70

Skua: 15, 27, 33, 45, 51, 75, 87
snakes: 70
Snowy Sheathbill: 75
Sooty Shearwater: 79
Spheniscidae: 3, 63
Spheniscus humboldti: see Humboldt Penguin
Spheniscus magellanicus: see Magellanic Penguin
Spheniscus mendiculus: see Galapagos Penguin
Sprattus fuegensis: 55
Teuthowenia sp.: 41
Themisto gaudichaudii: 41, 51
Thysanoessa gregaria: 41, 51
Thysanopsetta naresi: 32
Tierra del Fuego: 53
Todarodes fillippovae: 64
Tussac Grass: 34, 53, 60, 77, 78
vultures: 66
White-chinned Petrel: 79

ABOUT THE AUTHOR

Dr Mike Bingham has worked for the United States Government, British Government and Falkland Islands Government on a number of wildlife projects. Prior to 1993 Mike was working for the United States Government in Hawaii, helping to establish a research and banding programme for marine turtles. In 1993 Mike moved to the Falkland Islands to take up the Government funded post of Conservation Officer. Since then he has been studying penguins, and monitoring the effects of human activity, such as fishing, oil exploration, farming and tourism. His love of penguins and attention to detail has allowed him to explore the private life of penguins in a way that few others have achieved.

In 1995 Mike led an island-wide penguin census of the Falkland Islands which showed that populations had declined by over 80% since commercial fishing began. The Falkland Islands Government insisted that the declines were part of a global trend, so in 1996 Mike led a penguin census of the remainder of the world population, proving that populations were only declining in the Falklands.

When Mike refused to cover up his findings, he was kicked out as Conservation Officer. Since then he has set up the Environmental Research Unit, and continued his penguin research using independent funding.

In 1998 oil exploration began in the Falklands, and poor environmental protection led to three separate oil spills, killing hundreds of penguins and other seabirds. Mike protested about the lack of environmental safeguards, and the unnecessary damage being done to Falklands wildlife. The Falkland Islands Government decided that Dr. Bingham's research posed a threat to future wealth from fishing and oil development, and began a campaign to remove him.

Firstly Mike discovered firearms hidden under his bed, but fortunately was able to dispose of them prior to the Customs raid which followed. Then he was arrested on charges of deception, but released when the Police were forced to admit they had fabricated the evidence. Then the Falkland Islands Government tried to deport him, claiming that he had criminal convictions for burglary, which he didn't. The government were eventually forced to admit that they had used convictions belonging to a totally different person, and that another "administrative error" had occurred.

When Mike was arrested a third time, he turned to Amnesty International, who put him in touch with Index on Censorship. They exposed the corruption within the Falkland Islands Government, and the story hit the British newspapers in October 1999. The Sunday Times, The Guardian, The Observer, The Daily Post and Birdwatch magazine all published the story, with titles such as "Arrested, framed, threatened - Researcher fights a one-man war in the Falklands".

Despite their 4 year campaign of harassment, the Falkland Islands Government were forced to accept Mike's findings regarding penguin declines, and annual fishing effort has been reduced. Since then Gentoo and Rockhopper penguin populations have stopped declining, and now seem to have reached an equilibrium, albeit at a much lower level than before fishing began. Unfortunately Magellanic Penguins are still declining in the Falklands, and Dr. Bingham is now concentrating on identifying the cause, with support from the Chilean government. Sales from this book help fund this vital research.

Printed in the United States
95976LV00001B/23/A